At the Edge of the Abyss

Hal Saif

At the Edge of the Abyss

Unpostmodern Thoughts on Life, Death, and Culture

Hal Sarf, Ph.D.

CENTER FOR HUMANITIES
AND CONTEMPORARY CULTURE
Berkeley
2001

Copyright © 2001 by Hal Sarf

Library of Congress Cataloging-in-Publication Data

Sarf, Hal, 1941-
    At the edge of the abyss: unpostmodern thoughts on life, death, and culture / by Hal Sarf.
    p. cm.
    ISBN# 0-9676307-0-3
      1. Life. I. Title

BD431 .S2715 2000
191--dc21   00-045528

A Publication of the
Center for Humanities and Contemporary Culture
(A nonprofit educational organization)
P.O. Box 9716
Berkeley, CA 94709
(510) 845-4286
hsarf@chcc-edu.org
www.chcc-edu.org

Manufactured in the U.S.A.

REGENT PRESS
6020A Adeline Street
Oakland, CA 94608

Der gute Erzieher kennt Fälle, wo er stolz darauf ist, daß sein Zögling *wider ihn* sich selber treu bleibt....
A good educator knows cases in which he is proud of the fact that his pupil remains true to himself in *opposition to him*....

Zur Humanität eines Meisters gehört, seine Schüler, vor sich zu warnen.
It is part of the humanity of a master to warn his disciple about himself.

Es hilft nichts: jeder Meister hat nur einen Schüler–und der wird ihm untreu–denn er ist Meisterschaft auch bestimmt.
There is nothing to be done about it: every master has only one disciple–and he becomes disloyal to him–for he too is destined for mastership.

- Nietzsche

Contents

PROLOGUE
To My Readers / i

REFLECTIONS
Selves of Night and Day / 1
Writers and Words / 5
Socratic Rebellion / 10
Anger / 20
Encountering Death / 22
The Spectacle / 32
The Bow / 34
The Labyrinth / 35
Injustice / 38
Anxiety / 42
Altruism and Egotism / 47
Love, Eroticism, and the Abyss / 52
Memory / 58
Walking near the Abyss / 60

MOODS
Walking in Step with Life / 65
Spirit / 67
Where We Dwell / 68
Time's Duration / 69
Exuberant Life / 70
Wild Desires / 71
Destiny / 72

The Lovers / 73
Sorrow / 75
Daybreak / 76
Rapture / 78
Dawn / 79
You / 80
Signs / 81
Life / 82
Spider's Web / 83

KNOWING

A Report to the Children of the Planet Athanatos / 87
Halls of Academe / 99
Immediacy and Abstraction / 108
Precipice of Knowledge / 116
Masks of the Emerging Self / 120
Romantic Mysticism and the Real / 127
Parody of Postmodernism / 139
Postmodern Fallacies 1 / 144
Postmodern Fallacies 2 / 152

EPILOGUE

Walking My Path / 163

Prologue

To My Readers

At the Edge of the Abyss: Unpostmodern Thoughts on Life, Death, and Culture is a book of short essays, aphorisms, and poetic moods that, when viewed as a totality, are thoughts on issues of significance to me—and perhaps to any person who wonders about life, death, self-identity, God, love, justice, evil, and suffering. The book grew from years of immersion in, and reflection on, life's recurring paradoxes and challenges. Each section stands alone to be pondered in itself, and the work as a whole lacks a single thematic thread to link the parts into a definite sequential argument. The term "thought" traditionally signifies a type of reflection that is "meditative," "contemplative," "pensive," or a "flight of imagination."

Because *At the Edge of the Abyss* departs from the current climate of academic convention, I have identified myself as an "unpostmodern spirit." Indeed, one must be unfashionable—and even willfully rebellious—if philosophy is to regain its original purpose of provoking ordinary people to think seriously about issues that matter to their lives, especially in an age when philosophy is the preserve of a few highly trained academics who speak and write in specialized languages that border on being inaccessible jargon.

At the Edge of the Abyss is without a beginning, middle, and end because thinking itself is naturally fluid and akin to a circle. Any point of a circle can be arbitrarily conceived as a beginning, middle, or end, depending on how one defines it in relation to other points. Thinking is an endless process in which apparent endings—or firm conclusions—give rise to further perplexities and hence to new beginnings. In that respect, thinking which is true to its essential nature is never finished, because its source is that deep spring within the self from which arises a constant flow of images, feelings, and ideas that momentarily force themselves into conscious awareness. Taken together, the individual aphorisms, poems, and essays give a picture of my mind's workings and of my stance as a philosopher who makes no claim to offer certainty in a world that is wonderfully rich in paradox.

Meditative writers obviously require attentive readers who crave good books to stir their minds, but it is no easy task today for thoughtful writers and readers to find each other in order to share ideas fruitfully. This is particularly true in the present age, in which life is conducted at a furious pace that stifles the contemplative spirit, and in which both writers and readers are often at the mercy of the current *Zeitgeist* of market-driven values and facile, rapid solutions to serious cultural and personal issues that mirror our frenzied state of being.

Indeed, people today are often enmeshed in a complex web of duties and roles that cause them to feel anxious, fragmented, and receptive to a steady deluge of trendy, easily digested literature (fiction or nonfiction). Seeking to give people simplistic, reassuring conceptual and spiritual maps to guide their lives and abolish their confusion, such fashionable literature is designed to suppress the healthy suspicion of people that the world—and life itself—is terribly complex and deserving of sustained reflection. In writing *At the Edge of the Abyss* I invited both myself and my readers to slow down, to think grand ideas, and to once again dialogue about issues that have challenged thoughtful, liberally educated minds for millennia.

What exactly do I ask of *you*, my reader? That you receive my thoughts as gifts to examine and judge— be these provocative, rich, perplexing, unworthy, rebellious, or unfashionably traditional. Philosophizing for me—and perhaps for you as well—involves the Herculean feat of trying to articulate conceptually those experiences, thoughts, and feelings that are elusive and perhaps ultimately impenetrable. Indeed, thinking may lead one into dark caves where no light shows the way, but thinking may also help us ascend to mountain peaks where the sun burns brightly enough that the mind can clearly illuminate the objects and themes of its reflection.

If thinking is difficult and inviting of bouts of despair when challenged by mighty paradoxes, confusions, and contradictions, then the alternatives to thinking are either to fall into a mental torpor by succumbing to life's everyday duties and pressures, or to retreat into a mystic silence of direct insight that is beyond linguistic depiction. Meaningful conversation ceases in both cases.

Thinking that seeks to sail forth freely must first disentangle itself from the heavy chains that partisan interests forge to ensnare it, be these political parties, churches, governments, or fashionable cultural ideologies. Truth alone—not prudence, money, or acclaim—ought to be the exclusive guiding star of the philosopher.

At the Edge of the Abyss is my effort to plant a few thought-seeds, some of which may have matured into colorful, aromatic flowers that I ask you to behold and scent at your leisure. If the book helps you to slow down and think, then it serves its purpose. Feel free to place my work on your coffee table adjacent to your favorite easy chair for scrutiny when a reflective mood takes hold; or, if you prefer, on the mantel above the fireplace to allow quick disposal in a rapture of flames if my words fail to lighten your overburdened spirit.

I invite you, then, to spend some time aboard my ship, christened **Thought-Journey**, that sails on mind's restless currents to explore its vast, unknown territories, for which no official maps exist to pinpoint their exact locations or to illustrate the precise whereabouts of hazardous reefs that threaten our progress. Like life itself, thinking can be a dangerous voyage. If you decide to come aboard, then be prepared to meet an ominous swell or two, and perhaps even a hurricane that darkens the heavens with furious high winds and mighty downpours of rain that bring foreboding to the spirit. But also expect to encounter some glorious, sunny days when the exquisite sky and calm blue sea fill you with joy as the mind's eye unveils things in a new light. I promise to steer the ship as carefully as possible and ask no recompense for my effort other than sharing good conversation along the way.

REFLECTIONS

Selves of Night and Day

At still moments when my mind gains freedom from the manifold distractions and duties of everyday life, I sometimes ponder the meaning of that odd experience I have of swinging to and fro between two poles of self-identity. I name these identities the Self of Night and the Self of Day. Only when disciplined thought possesses me may the essential outlines of these seemingly contradictory selves be told in words and released from the dark mists of inarticulate feeling that envelop them.

I instantly know my Self of Night to be an unfathomable sea of speechless wisdom. It is a restless universe of swaying moods and feeling-tones of diverse colors; yet it is only there that I paradoxically find a holy stillness—a sense of perfection—insulated from the noisy chatter of daylight life with its incessant demands of hearing, vision, and touch that always enmesh me in the play of the world's cacophony.

Dwelling in a region beyond the personal experience of anyone else, and free from the shackles of time, space, and causality, my Self of Night is a mere conjecture to others, because they visualize my identity, as they inevitably must, through the filtering mediums of their own individual selves which always mix parts of themselves with my words, deeds, and bodily gestures.

Largely concealed from others, I experience my Self of Night as an indivisible whole that ceases to reveal itself once it is broken down into its constituent elements. Such a procedure transforms me into a different mode of being, that of a subject which observes both itself and external phenomena from a detached standpoint, as if these were just empirical objects to be described in their manifold traits of shape, density, color, or type of material.

The Self of Night, then, fuses feeling, cognition, intuition, and reason into an indivisible whole, so that they flow into one another like streams rushing into a vast ocean, losing their individual identities as their waters pour into the depths. Lacking any capacity to reduce itself to specific elements without leaving itself behind, the Self of Night cannot be equal to a mere sum of externally related parts, for it bridges the chasm that separates the subject from its sensible object—a chasm that makes it impossible to experience life as the unity of pure presence.

Departing from a daylight world that illuminates objects, events, and persons as distinct beings—a world whose reality depends on framing these as exterior things to be observed—I transform into the Self of Night which, in the immediacy of experience, sheds every mediation to discern the fullness of being ringing its gloriously holy tones—silently! It is then that I directly know myself to be the microcosm wherein the macrocosm truly dwells, and I break free from the prison bars that cleave me from both myself and world to attain that healing sense of unity that ends every self-division.

— ••• —

I too, inevitably, am my Self of Day that rises to awareness to claim my identity as regularly as the Sun emerges from the shrouds of dark night, for both refuse to be denied their eternal right. Illuminated by the day, I transform into a self who is largely mere surface to others, as they are to me. Indeed, I not only appear as a single person among countless, mostly anonymous others, but I also experience myself as a body susceptible to decay and death, being ruled by the mighty powers of space, time, and causality, which play both gently and harshly with me, as with every other finite being. Incessantly relying on cognitive maps drawn by culture to guide its life, my Self of Day tries to accomplish what is humanly necessary for existence by reducing all that is subtle, ambiguous, and overpowering to manageable proportions, so that it may get on with the business of living in an orderly manner.

To others, my Self of Day always appears as inseparable from the facts and events that distinctively enmesh me in the outer world's web. Indeed, the "others" want to know if I am married, divorced, or single, with children or without, what I do for a living, whether I dress well or sloppily, and how much property and money I have—as if these and other things could provide a window to the identity of my spirit! I am a being lacking in mystery to them, for they cannot possibly experience what it is I become when the rays of the daylight sun cease to shine on me, the time when I transform into the Self of Night that is invisible to everyone but me—and only to me in a directly knowing silence!

The Self of Day, then, is mere surface and fully visible, and if it is never more than it appears to be, it is describable only in a language shorn of poetic subtlety and mythic imagery. In fact, it experiences terror if told that its boundaries exceed the impressions given through sense-perception and the concepts that spring from these observations.

The Self of Day holds no true enigmas, uncharted regions, or deep wells; it is akin to a small and shallow lake that can easily be observed and surveyed in its volume, composition, life forms, and topography. As daybreak casts its first rays of light, the Self of Night disappears from view, retreating to that nameless place that is without fixed boundaries or definite shapes. That deep and mysterious self is a magnificent swirling sea of countless passions and secretive visions to which I succumb as night takes hold.

Writers and Words

Genuinely meritorious writers are driven to hold heartfelt inner dialogues about what they wish to say, and about how best to shape words to communicate the wealth of ideas and feelings they experience. Moreover, writers of integrity must endeavor to remain immune to the fickle influences of current literary fashions, to the temptation to compromise vision and honesty for the sake of gaining notoriety and money, and to any misguided prudence that avoids offending influential critics for fear of receiving unfavorable reviews.

These formidable forces tempt writers to distort their ideas and styles beyond recognition, to undermine their spontaneous and creative flow of words, and to abdicate their integrity in exchange for validation and income by becoming dependent on the whims and prejudices of the powerful. Writers ought to focus their mind's eye on stating the truth—that highest and rarest of virtues—as they perceive it, and their words should be meticulously woven to achieve the subtlety, power, and remarkable insight that moves others to see themselves and life from new perspectives.

Only after writers forge words into a concluding, though never perfectly satisfying form, are readers invited to enter their nuanced imaginative worlds of feelings, observations, and judgments to become both learners and critics. Still, finding appreciative critical readers is always an unexpected and happy finale to the struggle of writers to be heard, especially because the lives of both writers and readers are marked by daily anxieties, conflicts, and distractions that threaten to dissipate the concentration needed to spend time writing or reading books of integrity, strength, and depth.

The outer, worldly obstacles that great writers must overcome to fulfill their creative callings parallel their inner experience of strife, which originates in possessing a great diversity of rich and often contradictory voices that would pull their work in different directions. Self-mastery is needed to control and give rank order to the voices that compete for attention and the exclusive right to style words and ideas in their own images and resonances of feeling. Lacking such mastery, writers fall prey to indecision, dissipation of energy, and lack of clarity about what they intend to accomplish, let alone execute. The finished work, then, marks the victory of one commanding voice that suppressed its rivals by exiling them—momentarily!—to that shadowy, silent region of mind that perhaps is known only in dreams. When an outcast voice arises from the depths to take control, we witness the miraculous birth of a new writing project.

Persons who seriously encounter a writer of

genius become participants in another's bounteous inner dialogue, which is then felt to be their own as long as the word-enchantment lasts. Is a great creative work always marked by an uncanny and rare capacity to evoke in someone else a sorely needed conversation?

--- ••• ---

Writers of substance always embrace the intensity of life, for each day ushers in wondrous new moods, shades of color, and sounds to experience, from the elation born of dwelling on heights close to the sun's radiance that fill the spirit with sublime joy, to the dismal descent into gloomy valleys that darken the spirit and sap life's vitality. Readers are not always aware that writers are thankful for those mild and contented states of mind that balance the extremes. Without the solace of those middle places, the writer can neither tame the wildest passions nor gain sufficient self-presence to examine judiciously and calmly communicate in a fertile language the smallest details of life.

Some writers are blessed with a graceful ease of expression, as if the activity of translating thoughts into words is entirely unforced and guided by some relentless instinct akin to breathing, sexual union, or hunger. What appears to the reader to be a natural ease may conceal the fact that serious, probing writing is often a lonely activity stamped by hesitation and doubt. Lonely because the passion for reflection leads writers to experience an almost inhumanly cold detachment from life—the essential condition of allowing persons, events, and things to express their subtlety to the observing eye; and marked by hesitation and doubt because writers of merit are not always confident that language can do justice to the endless impressions and thoughts that stream through them, often in rapid succession.

For words must be judiciously chosen, lest reckless, imprecise expression invite readers to make wild claims about what the writer "really meant." But how can writers prevent readers from holding them responsible for saying things they did not mean, given that a degree of ambiguity is always present when words, written or verbal, are shared between persons? If language—at least language that attempts more than merely to transmit objective data—naturally requires interpretation, then sharp discrepancies may arise between the author's intention and the reader's understanding.

Although ambiguity cannot be eliminated even when language is made as precise as possible, it perhaps can be minimized when writers renounce the romantic illusion that ideas magically spring forth fully formed and intelligible to others from inspiration alone—as if they might forgo the hard discipline of careful, responsible word-sculpting of inspired but rough first impressions.

Inspiration by itself hardly guarantees lucid communication, although it is true that inspiration wells up from a home deep within the spirit, that place of shadowy impressions, rich feelings, and half-articulate ideas from which great writers unavoidably draw illumination and energy—often unknown to themselves! But writing entails the duty to rework inspired intuitions into carefully chosen words of expressive force to enable readers to journey to places they have not visited before, or at least help them see the familiar in a new way.

Above all, a writer should avoid deliberately confusing or deceiving the reader—unless confusion and deception are used as elements of style to prepare minds to shed rigid, timeworn habits. Still, regardless of a particular writer's talent and precision, his or her work remains at the mercy of the personal agendas, idiosyncrasies, insensitivities, and intellectual limitations of readers who can hardly avoid transforming the writer's intended meanings into what they want to see. Alas, the writer's dilemma not only points to the intrinsic risks of communication, but is symbolic of the human quandary of being forced to use words that have the effect of bringing us both closer and estranging us further.

Socratic Rebellion

If Socrates was a true rebel, then what obligations did that choice of life entail, and exactly how did his example inspire individuals throughout the ages to justify a stance of unyielding critical examination of the institutions, values, and life-practices of their communities?

Socrates said in the *Apology* that he served as a virtuous "gadfly" to the Athenians by "caring" for their souls. He claimed divine sanction from the Delphic oracle to pursue his cross-examining Athenians with reputations for wisdom to show they were truly ignorant about the natures of virtue, beauty, piety, courage, and justice. Preferring death to abandoning his philosophical vocation of unmasking pretended wisdom—and asking people to ponder how best to live—Socrates tried and failed to persuade his jury that his criticisms of Athenian institutions, traditional values, and ways of life were animated solely by a desire to improve both his city and its citizens.

Indeed, he justified his claim to be an unselfish man of virtue by pointing to his poverty, neglect of private affairs, refusal to take fees, and abstention from membership in any political party or interest group that might prejudice him. Although the evidence that Socrates gave to legitimize his vocation of "caring for souls" can be challenged, it remains the case (if Plato's depictions of his teacher are to be trusted) that his manner of living and dying gives plausibility to his self-understanding as a truth-seeker who found serious errors and contradictions in Athens' fabric of civic and private life.

Rebels who take inspiration from Socrates' example will likely experience similar difficulties to those that marked the philosopher's life. A person whose words and deeds are strongly critical of commonly accepted traditions, ethical precepts, and life-styles is always asking for trouble. Most people become defensive towards individuals who act as if they possess superior vision and moral character to themselves, and they wonder what gives the rebel the right to tell them why their lives are unhappy and confused—even if that is clearly the case. The rebel, then, is often experienced as a disruptive presence, although from his own perspective his strong criticism is essential to get people to examine whether their self-understandings embody faulty assumptions and unhealthy consequences for living.

Driven to unmask the social disguises that people often erect to hide their dissatisfaction, vulnerability, and confusion, and thinking that the quest for truth is the noblest of vocations, the rebel's critical words are akin to arrows that often miss their targets—the spirits of those he would awaken from a self-satisfying torpor. Threatened with exile as a perpetual stranger from the public world of sight and sound, the rebel often suffers from a lack of judicious, sympathetic regard; and if he is fortunate enough not to encounter a still more grievous fate, the rebel is merely written off as a disturbed and pitiful individual who is less a real threat than an object of curiosity and a candidate for psychotherapy.

If the rebel dwells in a stable, relatively conflict-free community, but refuses the tacit or overt expectation that he quell his anxiety-producing criticism, then he is often treated with silent neglect—a stance intended to make him ineffective. When the rebel's words are heard, it is usually for a brief moment or two because most listeners are too busy with their daily struggles to spend much time pondering his critical views. Besides, the majority of people are instinctively unsympathetic to the rebel because they find life more comfortable when they believe that their traditions, common sense, and political institutions deserve unquestioned loyalty and respect.

The object of sour glances and abusive whispers for trying to undermine the values and practices deemed essential to the ongoing identity of his community, the rebel's call to people to inspect earnestly their public and private lives is deflected by the twin obstacles of cowardice and fear. If "the silent treatment" fails to curb the rebel, then the next line of defense is for people to express angry disapproval in the hope of quelling his voice; and if these punishments prove futile in restoring comfort to the rebel's detractors, they can arrange to cut off his access to public forums or threaten his very survival by destroying his ability to earn a livelihood. Imprisonment or assassination are the weapons of last resort.

The rebel, then, finds it no simple matter to carry out his vocation as a conscience to the public world; and if he is a loner without the support of a small circle of like-minded friends who share a common critical project, then he faces the danger of experiencing a terrible isolation that easily breeds self-doubt. Lacking validation from others, the rebel may begin to question whether his against-the-grain views are actually truthful assessments of reality, and may even be plagued by the unsettling thought that perhaps he is demented because he rejects the values and conducts that the great majority find truly rewarding.

If the rebel lacks the ability to overcome the moments of self-doubt that may trouble him, then these may grow in strength to become an unyielding warning voice that stridently urges him to abandon his gadfly stance and be a sensible, prudent individual who adjusts to socially acceptable discourse and action. In all but the strongest, most independent spirits, the will to rebel can be broken by the common human desire to submit to institutional authority and public opinion to avoid the perils engendered by nonconformity.

Targeted for gossip and ridicule by his enemies who share glasses of wine in a comfortable and elegantly furnished living room, the rebel remains outside in the freezing cold rarely to be asked inside to share the warmth. Of course, he would refuse the invitation anyway, as is befitting a prophetic spirit who affirms that rejection and suffering are signs of his appointment to the special vocation of caring for souls.

— ••• —

What reasons lead the rebel to stand firm in his untimely convictions, to risk dangers to himself, and to forgo the ordinary human desires for security and acceptance that embracing consensual values and practices often engender? The rebel passionately affirms that life is hardly worth living if independent judgment and personal integrity are sacrificed in favor of elevating prudence to be the guiding star of life. Still, is not prudence necessary for self-protection in a social universe where people compete for scarce resources and are willing to lie, cheat, and manipulate others to realize their goals?

The prudent person not only hides his true feelings and agendas for fear of being vulnerable to harm by others who are willing to exploit weaknesses to advance themselves, but also carefully calculates the effects that words and deeds will likely have in a variety of social situations—with respect to work, family dynamics, friendships, and political activity. Modifying behavior to fit consensual standards and expectations, the prudent individual avoids being labeled a dissenting troublemaker as that would endanger career opportunities, validation by others, and material security. Prudence is certainly a virtue that fosters survival; yet it also can lead to serious compromises of core moral values, and to a deep division between how one appears to others and what one privately believes.

An excessively prudent person's words and deeds fail to reveal threads of moral consistency across diverse situations, and he is even akin to a chameleon that changes its exterior color and shape to blend innocuously into a variety of environments to avoid danger. Prudence as a way of life can lead a person to manifest incompatible—even blatantly contradictory—values, goals, and identities, at least when the diverse parts of a person's life are examined in terms of overall coherence.

Unlike the prudent individual, the rebel refuses to jeopardize moral integrity for the sake of security and social acceptance because these are of secondary value compared to living a life marked by courage, honesty, and devotion to civic and personal improvement. The true rebel is willing to embrace death and martyrdom—as did Socrates, Sir Thomas More, Martin Luther King, and Gandhi—to avoid any hypocritical splits between appearance and reality, or between word and deed.

The boundary between genuine and specious examples of Socratic rebellion can be difficult to fix with certainty. After all, an opportunistic individual may calculate that self-interest is best served by acting the part of a moralistic rebel in some situations—a facade that may conceal the fact that one is really an arrogant, power-hungry sophist who uses the rhetoric of virtue to manipulate others for personal benefit.

Still, there is one test to help distinguish between sophistic, deceptive rebels who claim they possess truth and virtue, and authentic rebels who feel certain of having a higher calling to improve the quality of life for both the individual and the community. Authentic rebels who conduct their lives in a manner that harmonizes with their moral values and goals, are ultimately willing to die for these rather then renounce their mission of "caring for souls," whereas false rebels not only contradict their words by their deeds, but they also readily change the character of their speech when comfort and self-interest dictates.

─── • • • ───

The authentic rebel firmly believes he possesses the necessary vision and moral fiber to serve as a penetrating light to help ordinary people perceive the contradictions and deficiencies that their values and conducts engender. Fearing to cultivate the *radical honesty* and *heartfelt perplexity* that are their birthright, the majority hesitate to share their doubts, anxieties, and confusions for fear of being seen as vulnerable, laughable, or just plain stupid. Besides, it is always safer to walk down well-trodden paths than to strike out in new directions.

Fated to say things that most prefer to relegate to silence for lack of candor and courage, the rebel, with his sharp questions and unsettling critical judgments, evokes in others a defensive anxiety that spawns the suspicion that he is a truly vain person whose views are biased, self-serving, and even dangerous. Despite that suspicion, the true rebel fails to claim that he possesses absolute truth; rather, he fully admits that no human judgments, however inspired and thoughtful, are fully immune to the subtle influences of emotional and intellectual bias. Still, his firm devotion to his vocation is justified by the powerful conviction that it is far better for one to accept the challenge to engage in self-examination than to live thoughtlessly by conforming to consensual standards without pondering their implications for self-identity.

Throwing caution to the wind, the rebel displays his imprudent ideas and judgments for all to see, and he is sometimes thought to be an immature, childish person who lacks any hint of restraint. For him, however, being a so-called adult is not very desirable if that means that opportunism, distrust, moral insensitivity, and defensiveness command the course of life. Fashioning an existence that thoughtlessly spends precious time pursuing the so-called "good" things—money, power, status, and security—makes little sense to the rebel, given his belief that a life of integrity demands being fully oneself, even if that means being termed a "loser" in the ceaseless competition for material rewards.

A talent for furthering self-interest by shrewdly

projecting insincere masks to deceive others not only entails hypocrisy—surely to be ranked among the worst of human vices—but rests on the dubious supposition that living well requires staying as hidden as possible in essential matters to avoid vulnerability to the intrigues of enemies. If honesty leads one to be exposed and predictable, then it would seem that only fools and martyrs unreservedly engage in truthful displays of themselves. Such reasoning legitimates mask-wearing by supposing that the supreme aim of life is to be a "winner" as defined by socially consensual standards of value.

Still, so-called winners may discover that their short-run gains actually sow the seeds of long-run defeat by transforming them into blatantly self-regarding, materialistic persons who lack much capacity for love, trust, or compassion. Their cynicism towards others may lead to an abiding feeling of emptiness and to an incapacity to grow by risking vulnerability. The rebel questions whether money, power, and status are the most worthy goals to pursue given the fact that possessing these fails to stave off the unsettling thoughts that death may suddenly take everything away and that life was wasted in trivial pursuits.

The rebel, then, is a person for whom candor is of the highest virtue. Candor is easily confused with vanity or a deliberate will to offend, although it is possible to think of candor as akin to a strong, penetrating light that jolts the eye habituated to seeing through dim shadows. One might think the rebel is overly harsh in his evaluations of people and society, and forgetful of Jesus' wise saying that it is best to "judge not lest ye be judged." That maxim makes perfect sense if followed with a sincere heart and without any hidden resentment, for it brings peace to the spirit by reconciling it to the stresses and injustices of existence that cause frustration, poisonous anger, and the will to retaliate. However, it must be admitted that the rebel is not sufficiently Christian to embrace Jesus' counsel, believing instead that righteousness and truth are of higher rank than unconditional forgiveness.

Anger

For all its appearance of negativity, anger can be a most healing emotion that releases frustrated energy and restores feelings of power and dignity after one suffers humiliation and defeat. Indeed, life's perpetual blows inevitably breed occasions for anger, except for persons so overwhelmed by the dissonances and sharp edges of life that they protect themselves by ceasing to feel strongly about practically almost anything and lose the will to express that special anger that says "no" to individuals and situations which thwart being fully oneself.

Anger and death are close relatives, and if death spoke to us, it would surely say: "Dearest brothers and sisters, you have supreme need of me: I am the force that spawns you into existence. And yet, paradoxically, you are nothing, because I am your supreme master. Whenever you think of the future, or reminisce about the past, or notice what the moment offers, you cannot fail to observe my perpetual intimations of demolition. You shudder when I issue signs that my terrible embrace is drawing near, and you are eternally perplexed by the question of why you fall under my power."

Anger springs from being enmeshed in webs of necessity woven by one's own intemperate desires and foolish hopes, by selfish intrigues launched by others, and by those uninvited, abrupt events that ruin security and plans for happiness. If death's handiwork hems us in, and if we reel from the wounds, weariness, and decay of unrelenting daily struggle, then anger is a suitably judicious rejoinder to being players in a game we cannot possibly win.

And yet, although angry eruptions provide brief relief and pleasure, these victorious moments soon succumb to the melancholic insight that death is our eternal lover, one that no power tears asunder.

Encountering Death

Common opinion has it that death is a very great evil, being that terrifying ruling power which the frail human will can neither banish as a haunting presence nor negotiate with when the fated moment of finality approaches. Death never seems inclined to make exceptions to its single-minded mission of eventually transforming everyone—whether high or low, good or evil, young or old, beautiful or ugly of form—into eternal dust. Decay and termination reign victorious over the force that brings us into life.

The individual spirit, knowing itself only as a living center of thought and action inhabiting a world rich in colors, shapes, and sounds, and populated by a diversity of organic and inanimate beings, feels intense perplexity, and often recoils in horror, when it ponders the future certainty of its own demise. The plausible speculation that the world and other people continue to exist after one's own death provides little consolation when the self tries to imagine the unthinkable, namely, the *condition of its being devoid of thought and feeling*, indeed, of *personal identity* and control over its own fate. Pondering its *own* inevitable non-being, the self encounters a mystery it cannot possibly penetrate.

One way to mitigate the fear and perplexity that envelops the thought of non-existence is to believe that every individual possesses a soul that survives the empirical termination of bodily functioning. That is why ardent practitioners of the great Western religions of Judaism, Christianity, and Islam believe that death is neither a great evil nor the final cessation of life; instead, it is the moment of the immortal soul's transition to a heavenly world in which every woe, confusion, and fear is eternally left behind, at least for the righteous whose earthly lives harmonized with God's plan. And even if it is believed—as the Hindus and Buddhists teach—that each person possesses an immortal soul that transmigrates to another body and life until final release from the Wheel of Karma, there is still the possibility that such a view—and the Western ones as well—is little more than a comforting illusion spawned by fear of the unknown.

—— ••• ——

Allow me to conjecture that death is a void that, by definition, is without the dimmest possibility of sensation, the slightest hint of personal identity, the minute awareness of other people, or any feeling whatsoever of being in a world. If true, then the condition of death is nothing to fear, and perhaps is best seen as a dreamless sleep—as Socrates stated in the

Apology when contemplating the meaning of his own impending demise—and a plausible alternative to the Orphic view that upon death the soul transmigrates from body to body in its unending sojourn from one existence to the next.

Assuming that death is nothing more than a state of absolute non-existence, it follows that anticipating this state—for example, on suddenly learning that one has a terminal illness—naturally fosters feelings of anxiety and even terror. Still, it is possible for some individuals to transcend momentarily these feelings to experience deeply the colors, tastes, sights, and sensations of life before these finally pass away, refusing to become either passively resigned or filled with horror. Paradoxically, the human capacity to anticipate death stems from the fact that the signs of death are everywhere to behold in the midst of life. Indeed, death's companions and heralds, whether accident, illness, or aging, serve to remind us of our ephemerality as we walk toward a future that may never actually arrive, since fate may strike us down before we go very far.

Excessive concern with death easily thwarts the spirit of life. It fills the self with dread about an event that is yet to present itself; dulls the capacity to experience the fullness of love, joy, beauty, and friendship when these come our way; mitigates against tasting the subtleties of well-prepared, finely spiced dishes and excellent vintage wine; and binds the self in the double chains of hopelessness and torpor, which undermine its belief that there is some good reason to live—leaving it to stew in the thought that perhaps death is welcome as absolute relief from its incessant misery.

If one is not to be overwhelmed by the morbid anticipation of death—especially if one finds neither solace nor truth in the idea of a soul that survives earthly termination to journey to some other time and place—then it is best to shift perspective and cultivate the smiling recognition that death is really an excellent friend, whose presence should spur us to embrace life with the intensity it deserves, especially since our earthly existence is all that we know and will likely ever have.

The abstract truth that life is finite in duration should not breed debilitating despair; after all, despair is but one feeling out of many that spring forth in the lively play of dark and light moods that possess us as we go about living. If a divine being exists, whoever or whatever it might be, it is inconceivable to me that such a deity dwells in a transcendent sphere utterly separate from our bodies, feelings, or thoughts—or from the nearly infinite variety of other life forms that populate the Earth as witnessed by our sense organs. Perhaps we ought to rejoice in the possibility that God is immanent in beings both large and small, and that we are participants in a larger life that is visible only after we learn to remove the dark clouds that shroud our inner sight.

What now is passing through you as an awareness, be that a thought, image, feeling, memory, or expectation, inhabits no other sphere of being but the pure present. There is only presence and nothing else. Concerns you have about what happened yesterday or might occur tomorrow only exist in the immediacy of your "now," for it is only when temporality is abstractly divided into distinct horizons of experience that past and future come into being to possess our attention. Death, then, does not exist until it *actually* occurs, although a self can be mired in the anticipation of it to such a degree that its ability to embrace fully the present is utterly thwarted.

Lacking awareness of eventual nullification by death, the human order as we know it would no longer be recognizable, for being finite is the essential root of our experiences of danger, regret, anxiety, loss, love, compassion, hope, and achievement. These experiences accompany us as we tarry in the uncanniness of a journey toward a finality that began the very instant we awoke to life in daybreak's miraculous light.

——— ••• ———

The wish to ensure personal survival by exiling death from its perpetual work of dissolution is certainly an age-old dream of mankind. The great Western religious faiths, whether Judaism, Christianity, or Islam have valiantly defended us against the terrifying thought that existence ends in non-being. And although scientific materialism has bred a profound skepticism toward the veracity of religious-philosophical ideas of "spirit," "soul," "God," "afterlife," and "heaven and hell," that hardly means that our modern "enlightenment" does not express in its own way mankind's ancient hope to overcome death.

Scientific advances in the fields of biological chemistry, genetics, and physiology have brought us to the brink of a new historical age when it might be possible through cloning and other techniques to engineer extremely long-lived humans, to banish the most ravaging diseases, and to rid our lives of anxiety and depression through the use of psychotropic chemicals. It would seem that modern science, for all its anti-metaphysical pretensions, is still driven by a powerful religious-moral imperative to abolish death and illness from our condition. And by unlocking the gate that reveals the path to immortality, science could finally relegate traditional religion and myth to the level of fantasies that offer solace but no true overcoming of death.

Let's suppose that human ingenuity reached the point of being capable of exiling death from our midst. Would that fantastic achievement be a glorious gift that truly benefited humankind, or would it leave us in significant respects in a far worse condition? Would it be best to reject that gift even if that meant continuing to have perishable bodies subject to pain, injury, and decay, to say nothing of the panorama of mental disorders, whether depression, anxiety, schizophrenia, paranoia, or mania, that might otherwise be defeated? And would living forever remove the causes of famines and wars, abolish the impulse of people to inflict emotional injuries on their fellow creatures whether through prejudice or insensitivity, or free us from sadness when our hopes for the future fail to materialize?

No doubt a world without death would have obvious advantages: we would neither feel horror and sadness at the passing of a sweet child inflicted with a rare malignant cancer, nor know the loss of our dear mothers, fathers, and friends that brings us to despair as we cannot prevent their minds and bodies from painfully disintegrating before our eyes. And would not such a world also offer everyone as much time as needed to pursue whatever projects thought worthy, whether gaining and enjoying material things, embracing friendships and love relationships, or cultivating personal creativity?

Although some forms of evil and suffering would undoubtedly fade away if death were abolished, I still think that the costs would decisively outweigh the benefits, not the least being that we would likely cease to be human beings in any traditionally recognizable way. Alas, a new and far less interesting species of life might spring forth, or alternatively, we would find ourselves having endless time to express our ordinary and contradictory human qualities—whether jealousy, competitiveness, egotism, deception, lust for power, violence, and hatred or self-sacrifice, compassion, love, integrity, nobility, and cooperation.

The anticipation and inevitability of death are what make us truly human and condition almost every shade of good and evil. Imagine a world without bodily decay, without the sad recognition that loved ones must inevitably depart, without that productive anxiety that spurs us to actualize our personal goals before we are struck down, and without the drive to create works of music, painting, sculpture, or architecture. Would not all of these wither for lack of a motivating impulse born of the insight that, because we are intrinsically fragile and ephemeral, it is wise to strive to leave something of ourselves behind that mattered to us and is memorable to others?

Indeed, could we love, be moved to joy, shed tears of grief, or sincerely sympathize with a friend's misfortune if a deathless, illness-free world came to be, with few if any occasions to experience either emotional or physical suffering? Above all, the capacity to love profoundly would greatly dim, because the depth of feeling we have for others is enriched and strengthened by the dreadful possibility that they may suddenly become ill and disappear from our lives in an unwelcome night of death.

And if we endured forever, or even for a much greater time than is currently possible, would not many things of great value largely dissipate in significance? Would we not lose the impulse to keep our promises; to offer a heartfelt apology to those we injure in the hope of receiving their forgiveness to lift our burden of guilt; or to strive to discern the boundaries between virtue and vice in an effort to decide how best to cultivate moral excellence in our brief time on Earth? The fact that we must decay and pass away brings meaning to our moral choices, ways of living, personal relationships, and hopes for the future.

My basic point should be obvious. Human life as we know it is marked by sharp and subtle contrasts of feeling, thought, and judgment—be these of wellbeing, illness, sexual passion, beauty, anxiety, conflict, depression, ugliness, or good and evil. Lacking the incessant play of these experiences, life would lose its inherent colorful contrasts of peaks and valleys and fade to a shade of monochrome gray. Indeed, there would neither arise any strong need to give rank order to the various possibilities for living that confront us, nor would it matter much if we abdicated responsibility for the effects that our choices had on others. Absent the reality of death's non-negotiable presence, life would no longer be an exhilarating journey of supreme personal significance marked by many challenges and uncertain outcomes. Yes, we belong to the empire of death, and without its lurking presence there would be no true stimulus for living.

Egotism, opportunism, deception, and the unrelenting quest to attain as much money and property as possible are the means that some people use to fill their spiritual void and to attain what turns out to be an ephemeral security in a world where sickness and death may strike unexpectedly. They may come to lament, at the approach of death, their past failures to enrich their moral and intellectual gifts and to have touched others deeply by offering friendship and love.

Cultivating a philosophical sensitivity is needed to embrace Sophocles' wisdom that we are "creatures of a day"—indeed, a wisdom that counsels us to recognize that life's tentative and obscure nature is an invitation to exist fully and to feel the wonder and anxiety that humbles human vanity, quells the evil of insensitivity to the suffering of others, and punctures the illusion that death only comes for others but never for oneself.

The Spectacle

Our human world—the amphitheater where our individual and collective spectacles unfold—is encircled by deep and shallow oceans, blue lakes, and muddy rivers; by rain, wind, and snow; by a variety of earth aromas; by magnificent rainbow colors; by sun, moon, planets, and stars that are tiny specks in a vast swirling cosmos; and by an endless multitude of living things, both great and small. As we strut about our little world, often feeling alone and confused in mind's twilight of dark and light shades, we enact our unique comedies and dramas, and even display to others a confident mask of knowing who we are, where we are, and how best to live—if only in public!

The whole spectrum of human virtues and vices is present in our small universe—from nobility, self-sacrifice, courage, honesty, compassion, moderation, justice, and love to cruelty, deception, egotism, fear, and the abuse of power. We are actors in a play for which we did not write the script, fated to perform our appointed roles according to obscure necessities which drive us on; and conceivably it is both a blessing and tragic fate that we cannot discern the identity of the playwright or his-her-its purpose in giving rise to life's drama and our individual places in it. Perhaps it is best not to probe too deeply into matters that we are not meant to know, at least if we lack the courage to embrace the unseen dangers and hardships that may unexpectedly appear.

Feeling naturally uncertain about our own and the world's design, we move from bouts of despair over our unhappy and strange condition to moments in which we feel able to decipher the plan that resides in the ground of Being, for we are sufficiently vain to believe that either reason or revelation will unlock the deepest secrets.

Possibly the truth is located in a region between the two. Perhaps we are permitted only to have fleeting, inexact images of, and insights into, ourselves and the nature of things, although as a species we are too arrogant to admit that certain knowledge of the totality is beyond our ken. And thank some unknown deity for that, or else philosophers would lack all impulse to keep searching!

Still, it is amazing that we humans, having been catapulted into our body-houses by an unknown author who dwells in a "somewhere" we cannot visit while we live, feel compulsively driven to solve the riddle of our appearance from the darkness into the light of life.

The Bow

Heraclitus taught that life is akin to a bow stretched in great tension. When a certain limit is passed, the bow may break, and destruction ensues. Although that limit is difficult to discern, given that existence is an obscure experiment, there is little doubt that the fullness of life is found only at the limit close to where doom resides. Seeking that limit entails the experience of strife, and strife inevitably brings suffering, for the more we embrace life in all its problematic qualities, depths, and enriching wonders, the more we encounter contradiction.

To traverse life in a manner that avoids the pain of contradiction, and that forgoes embracing paradox, are marks of a cowardly and small spirit. Life is richest when there is animated conversation between the polar voices dwelling in spirit. Our task is to harmonize these or else risk destruction. A peace treaty is necessary to give each a just place in the whole. Still, peace is a momentary respite from the eternal strife of Being, indeed, of one's own being as well.

The Labyrinth

The self drifts in a sea of anxiety, carried along by irresistibly powerful currents toward jagged rocks. It is a rare individual who finds life's meaning in the allotted time before encountering destruction. And yet the inevitable fate that awaits the self is mostly concealed from it, for it has confidently erected mental dams and dikes that foster the illusion that it is well protected against the fury of life's dangerous currents. And it is often true that when strong currents suddenly appear to disturb the mind's tranquillity, these usually do not circulate very far to cause much havoc, although it is always the case that the self will eventually succumb to that special current of unyielding pressure that collapses its defenses.

What we commonly judge to be empirically real is always conditioned by prior acts of mind that spawn boundaries and identities from the primordial and inchoate mass of sensory experience. Actuality is composed of nothing more than mind's orderly weavings, embodied in a language that directs judgment and perception and that demarcates "reality" from fantasy. Statements about what is "real" reveal much more about typical forms of consciousness than about the objective world. Indeed, the general categories of objectivity and subjectivity, as well as the specific ways boundaries are drawn between the two, cannot be properly understood without examining mind's diverse patterns of spawning identities. But how does mind spawn a world that is felt to consist of a domain of beings separate from itself?

——— ••• ———

The self dwells in a labyrinth of many passages that it traverses until death, and, while it lives, it can neither leave the maze in which it finds its limits and possibilities, nor can it eliminate the traits of character that are etched into its being. That we know our way about the labyrinth should not surprise us. Our inherited, common culture teaches us habits of perception, goals to pursue and avoid, and meanings which regulate our relations to nature, to each other, to God, and to institutions. Culture, then, provides us with a large and detailed map that enables thought and action to be guided by common standards, and that ensures that we experience our collective world as predictable and stable.

So our map of the labyrinth—created by culture—is composed of busy roads and quiet byways on which we traverse through life. Culture not only provides the basic blueprint for our conviction that we know what exists to be encountered, perceived, desired, feared, and avoided, but also teaches us to distinguish the boundaries between reality and illusion. Perhaps persons we call "geniuses" are gifted with the uncanny ability to rethink and redraw those boundaries and maps.

Injustice

One of life's great discords is the fact that it fails to bestow good fortune equally to everyone, signifying perhaps that injustice is woven into the very fabric of existence. When observing the vast panorama of human life, we readily notice that natural inequalities of intelligence, motivation, and longevity are ubiquitous, causing handicaps to some people in the competition for security, status, and happiness. Fate decrees that some persons are born into impoverished circumstances, are raised by abusive, unloving parents, and are exposed to incompetent, neglectful teachers—all of which taint the experience of life with involuntary pain and misfortune.

Some people die hungry and poor, neglected by the ostentatious rich who might help them but hardly care; other individuals, famous for their achievements, suffer unexpected personal tragedies that burden their spirits and prevent them from reaching still greater heights. Still others, innocent of inflicting any harm, die all too young of painful diseases, bestowing in their brief stay only a few moments of joy on their parents and friends before being ripped away by a seemingly unjust fate. A lucky few progress to a materially secure golden old age, filled with smiles of contentment that disguise to themselves and others the deception and manipulation they used to catapult themselves to the top of the ephemeral heap.

It appears that life itself is beyond good and evil, because moral persons sometimes suffer evil fates despite their virtues, whereas base, calculating individuals who treat others as objects may gain fame and money and have long, healthy lives.

Most people, however, pass their lives neither inflicting great evils on others nor showing a capacity for exemplary goodness. Instead, they show little inclination to ponder their lives to discover what is truly valuable to pursue in their earthly stay, pass rather unnoticed through the world, and fail to touch others sufficiently to be worthy of special remembrance. Moments of happiness and pain alternate in every life, in varying degrees of intensity and duration, while death indiscriminately shadows everyone, adamantly refusing to exempt any individual from knowing its penetrating terminal gaze that transmutes life into dust—whether that person be poor or rich, ugly or beautiful, stupid or intelligent, weak or powerful, or painted in skin-shades of black, white or yellow.

But it is futile to measure our fates against those of others, since we will always find our own wanting in some crucial respect—a sure formula for feeling resentment and sorrow. The inclination to compare one's life to others often grows from a decided lack of self-respect—an inability to be at home with oneself—and from lacking culturally desirable traits or possessions, whether beauty, intelligence, creativity, love, moral virtue, power, wealth, or health.

If being flawed and unfulfilled in some respects is everyone's lot, then we should ideally embrace who we are—assuming we cannot overcome our limitations—to quell the growth of self-pity and to dispel the unproductive illusion that it would be better to be more like someone else, which is a certain recipe for self-hatred. Recognizing and embracing our imperfections is perhaps wiser and more noble than turning discontent into envy of, and bitterness at, others, as if our difficulties are always caused by egotistic, bad people who gain life's good things by conspiring to keep us down. The gift of life carries no intrinsic guarantee of being pain-free or joyful, or fulfilling of every desire with little or no resistance.

Perhaps it is best to smile when others think you less than themselves, for often their own lives are driven by the dubious belief that outdoing others in the struggle for property, power, and status might outwit death and confer immortality. It is superficial to measure success and personal worth in terms of money, property, and reputation, because obtaining these may require severe compromises of moral integrity, such as deceit, hypocrisy, and disloyalty to friends and family—at least when their pressing needs are perceived to drain time and energy from pursuing one's own self-interest. Indeed, persons who reveal an excessive impulse to accumulate material things to impress others often look to the outside world to fill the emptiness within, having shirked the responsibility to question the values and the meanings of their lives.

Anxiety

The widespread reliance on antidepressant and anxiety-reducing drugs to foster feelings of well-being, and to safeguard workplace efficiency against disruption, grows from a culture single-mindedly devoted to the ideal of eliminating physical and emotional pain from its midst. The drive to conquer pain is often justified as a compassionate moral duty, even though countless animals are maimed or destroyed in experiments designed to find drugs to combat wasting diseases and to extend indefinitely the human life-span. The great majority of people living in advanced technological societies, especially those with chronic, disabling diseases, want to make their lives as comfortable and pain-free as possible.

Although no right-thinking person would deny it is absolutely necessary to develop drugs that relieve the most excruciating physical and emotional discomforts—especially for the dying and for extreme cases of emotional distress where danger to oneself and others is involved—perhaps our culture has gone too far in attempting to remove pain from our midst, as if all forms of mental and physical discomfort refuted the value of existence and therefore should be totally banished from the human condition.

The issue is whether emotional and physical pain plays an essential role in enriching the experience of living. Pre-scientific cultures not only lacked our sophisticated pain-killing drugs, but people experienced sickness, death, and communal crises as intrinsic to an order of being that fated earthly life to be dangerous and tentative. Pain was an omnipresent reality, neither easily eliminated nor considered a refutation of the value of life. Instead, pain had symbolic meaning: it signaled a disturbance in the harmonious relationship between the gods and the human order, a disturbance that was both a warning and a call to restore harmony through religious ritual, sacrifice, and prayer. In short, pain and suffering had moral, religious, and metaphysical meaning that invited the self and the community to take decisive action.

What most disturbs people today about pain is the outbreak of anxiety that inevitably accompanies it. If illness signifies the breakdown of healthy organic functioning, and if our civilization has ceased to give such breakdown a metaphysical or religious significance—treating it as a sheerly physical event generated by biological, genetic, or chemical causes—then infirmity naturally triggers a mental image of *impending doom*, conceived as a horrifying cessation of consciousness rather than a transition to another form of existence. Death is viewed as an absurd, irrational event that ought to be abolished through the application of scientific knowledge.

Illness and pain, then, are greatly intensified by anxiety, that most unpleasant foreboding of the annihilation of self; and these are the very things which scientific culture feels compelled to eliminate to fulfill its Faustian vocation of mastering and reshaping both human nature and the cosmos. Only anxiety, pain, illness, and death—the last being the most elusive and incalculable in meaning—remain barriers to man's attempt to shed his age-old identity as an ephemeral and suffering creature and to become godlike.

——— ... ———

Anxiety is rooted in the presentiment that death is our fate—death being that most unwelcome power that shadows the living to fulfill its single vocation: to restore each living being to the unconscious oblivion from which it strangely emerged into the light. Unless death and illness are eliminated, there is no true cure for the ravages of anxiety, which erupts uninvited into our daily pursuits despite efforts to conceal it by losing ourselves in work, family affairs, and social encounters, or by projecting hopes for a better future that, in truth, may never arrive.

The drive to minimize or abolish anxiety and pain through chemical means and psychological therapies rests on a refusal to embrace a basic truth of the human condition, namely, that it is finite in nature. Anxiety, whether brought on by physical or emotional stress is, at bottom, the *premonition of final ending*, and without it we would lack the impulse to wonder about our lives as a whole, about the identity of the order of Being in which we participate, and about what values and goals we ought to pursue in the brief interlude between appearing and disappearing. Without anxiety, the root impulse for artistic and philosophical creativity would shrivel, and the primary good of life would be the pursuit of a variety of immediate pleasures.

If the self could detach itself momentarily from its everyday concerns to gain a clear vision of existence as a whole, it would surely see that it is nothing more than a vanity, an ephemeral and conflict-ridden being that is eternally under death's dominion. The self's drive to master anxiety and sickness is born of an illusory wish to transcend finitude. Rebelling against its inherent limits, it often wastes its gift of life by pursuing power, security, and wealth as the highest goals—as if such transient things might stave off its end!

Perhaps it is best to acknowledge anxiety as part of the inexorable ebb and flow of our beings, and thus to recognize that we always walk hand in hand with death; and if anxiety signals the premonition of death but not its actual condition, then we should embrace it as necessary to life while striving to examine ourselves in an effort to distinguish what is meaningful and fulfilling from that which is superficial and empty in the time allotted to us.

It is wise to converse with death. In doing so, we experience the exhilaration and despair of a life that is akin to walking on narrow mountain paths at the edge of a precipice. After all, life is inevitably a journey towards finality, but that knowledge should increase the depth and power of the fascinating interludes along the way. Indeed, perhaps death is a friend, the beneficent boatman who carries us over to the "other side," where we may learn of the source from which we sprang.

Is it not consoling to recognize that equality before the ruling power of death abolishes every division created by human vanity and artfulness? Know yourself to be the offspring of a boundless energy, sharing its passion to create and destroy, for it is both love and hate, and it seeds us with its own affliction. Give thanks that you are catapulted into the stream of life and are blessed with the capacity to experience joy and wonder; and finally, embrace your anxiety as a call that reminds you of your highest task, namely, to discriminate the essential from the trivial in a life that is nothing more than a brief if fascinating interlude.

Altruism and Egotism

It seems sensible to acknowledge that dealing with others in a spirit of fairness and equality can only be conditionally actualized, because no person is motivated by purely selfless impulses. Therefore, it is prudent to be wary of individuals who proclaim they are truly just, loving, and altruistic. You may find out later, sometimes at a great personal cost, that their noble utterances masked entirely self-regarding agendas. Even when manifesting love and virtue, people usually expect obvious or subtle benefit to themselves, whether that benefit be assessed in short or long time frames.

And there is always the risk that calculating benefits to oneself for dispensing good deeds may prove inaccurate because one's judgment is compromised by faulty logic, wishful thinking, or blind emotion. That partly explains why people are inclined to modify or break promises when it dawns on them that their original projections of benefit may turn out badly. No wonder there are so many lawsuits clogging the courts, and still more lawyers waiting in the wings eager for clients to give them fat retainers to obtain the justice they self-interestedly think they are due.

What an individual often sees as a just resolution of a conflict is rarely the result of a sincere and fair-minded evaluation of the situation. Nearly always, the influences of personal vanity, considerations of material advantage, and the pleasurable fantasy of getting even with someone—who is rightly or wrongly seen to have inflicted some small or great injury—affect one's perceptions.

Persons, then, manifest a strong tendency to place their own desires, interests, and security above those of others, at least in situations where helping another would bring harm to oneself. Seemingly altruistic actions usually turn out to be the result of self-interested motives at play. Mere instances of cooperation ought not be confused with altruism, since the former results from an assessment by both parties that mutual benefit would accrue from taking account of each other's wishes. Cooperation is most likely when both parties have roughly equal power and favors to bestow; that is why the rich help each other and not the poor to any great extent, unless their so-called altruism carries favorable tax breaks for them.

Also, excessive pain or weariness with life may motivate what appear to be altruistic, self-sacrificial acts. Upon close inspection, these good deeds may be motivated by the egotistic wish to shift attention away from one's own misery by strongly identifying with the misfortunes of another. Suicide, which may appear to be a noble sacrifice to rid oneself and others of a useless burden, may in fact be a supremely selfish act. Feeling utterly desolate, and thinking that one's life is "no damn good" to oneself or others, may engender a certain perverse pleasure at contemplating the final release from misery, because it is imagined that oblivion is much more desirable than a life of suffering.

Perhaps we need not definitively decide whether human beings are essentially selfish or altruistic, hateful or benevolent, violent or peace-loving, sensual or spiritual, evil or good. Simplistic choices are rarely true to the complexity of reality. People tend to be subtle mixtures of pettiness and generosity, cowardice and courage, hate and love, rudeness and sensitivity, deceit and honesty, and selfishness and self-sacrifice. These and other traits often combine indivisibly in each individual, and tend to shift their relative weights and modes of expression in response to changing situations. If one penetrates deeply enough, one will readily see that people in truth are not only fascinating composites of good and bad character traits, but are often inwardly confused, conflicted, and uncertain about their values and life-goals.

And because most people are naturally concerned with their own survival and happiness in a universe of scarce, unequally distributed resources, there are good grounds for treating each other with some degree of fear and suspicion—to say nothing of the conflicts that arise between people from their cultural differences of values, ideas, and goals, and ultimately from their possessing separate bodies. Still, it is an unhappy fact of life that we feel compelled, for the sake of self-protection and efficient living, to make swift, relatively fixed, and often unjust judgments about people we encounter given our lack of willingness and time to explore the unique qualities of our companions on the ship of life. We tend to be gracious, intimate, and supportive with friends while formal and protective of our privacy with strangers.

People want to feel secure, respected, productive and, above all, to believe that their lives are improving. Hence, they do not take kindly to criticism that undermines their judgments about their abilities, virtues, relationships, and plans for the future. Few people cultivate sufficient self-knowledge and courage to stand firm in the face of criticism without becoming anxious and defensive. Most find comfort in constructing their self-identities by conforming to consensual social values and practices, which provide them with maps of what to pursue and avoid. They shun intense self-examination for fear that it might cast a negative light on their habits of valuing, thinking, and acting, and reveal them to be more conformist and less independent than they wish to believe they are.

Finding it difficult to discard the social pretenses that their lives are relatively stable, comfortable, and progressing according to plan, people tend to avoid sharing their inevitable experiences of confusion, suffering, and forlornness because they dread admitting being needy and vulnerable. Individuals who appear needy, dependent, and overly anxious justly fear being shunned or ridiculed—for most people prefer to avoid disrupting their own lives by being drawn into a morass of problems they cannot solve—although people will generally be helpful as long as the cost to themselves is not too high.

The Christian moral ideals of loving one's neighbor as oneself, and doing unto others as you would wish them to do unto you, are prescriptions that rarely describe how life is generally conducted. It is quite difficult to be truly loving and forgiving of persons who exploit our vulnerabilites when we are dependent on them to meet our drives for survival, career advancement, and emotional well-being. As social life engenders sharing a common existence, the door opens to various types of servitude, conflict, frustration, and compromise, as well as to possibilities for fulfillment, trust, love, and virtue. But perhaps it is better to suffer the ambiguity of involvement than to foster an extreme protectiveness of spirit that easily hardens into a cold life of empty isolation and regrets.

There is little doubt that the human condition would be vastly improved if persons would mitigate their fear of being vulnerable and would, instead, voice their anxieties and problems to each other in an effort to overcome their isolation and share their common suffering. Even if nothing was solved, at least there would develop strong bonds of community and heartfelt conversation to pass the time before death inevitably arrives to solve absolutely the problems of living.

Love, Eroticism, and The Abyss

What is most difficult for me—and not just for me!—is giving and receiving love. As with every subtle, problematic, and powerful human emotion, love has many meanings, ones that the ancient Greeks especially pondered and voiced in refined distinctions, whether the feeling of non-erotic mutual attraction between friends (*Philia*), the restless desire for sexual pleasure between the two sexes and among members of the same sex (*Eros*), and the love that is entirely spiritualized, raising vision from the bodily, earthly domain to contemplation of the eternal beauty and harmony of the divine sphere (*Agape*).

Cynically speaking, people often justify their mutual erotic attraction by calling it "love," as if animal naturalness need be dignified by appeal to a word with a lengthy lineage of spiritual-moral meaning. This is especially true in the Christian tradition, which judges that the cultivation of an ethereal, otherworldly love saves the soul from the obsessive delights of the animal-erotic drive, which it views as the offspring of sinful temptation to be avoided as the devil himself unless sanctified by marriage vows that legitimate copulation only as a procreative necessity.

Slighted is the raw Freudian truth that what often lies at the root of love is mutual neediness, fear of loneliness, and the craving for libidinal pleasure; and only after these are sublimated into secondary objects—such as work, aesthetic creativity, and codes of law—does civilization take root. And with that, *Eros* is transformed into less disruptive expressions, whether spiritual love or an abstract, ideal love of humanity.

Freud may be only partly right in judging that love in all its myriad forms grows from a powerful primary libidinal instinct for pleasure which, for him, unfolds in a developmental sequence beginning with the oral phase, progressing through the anal one, and reaching culmination in the normal adult experience of seeking genital gratification with sexual partners of the opposite gender. If love, for Freud, is identified at bottom with the drive for pleasure, then there is always a narcissistic element in loving because one gives satisfaction to another not from an impulse of egoless altruism but from an expectation that an equal or greater amount of pleasure will be forthcoming. Thus, loving is possible only on condition that the implicit contractual obligation to satisfy and be satisfied is largely met by both parties. Lacking that, love must decay.

But does Freud have it right if he fails to acknowledge any ontological boundary between the quest for pleasure and the nature of love? And further, is it problematic to think that so-called higher forms of love, such as altruism, empathy, and compassion, are in the final analysis sublimations of an entirely self-regarding instinctual drive?

——— ••• ———

Consider the question of love from another angle of vision. The Christian tradition claims that genuine love is worlds removed from any pagan, animal quest for bodily pleasure; instead, love is present when the self, which is created by God in his image, cultivates its spiritual nature and experiences itself as utterly dependent on a transcendent ground of being.

Further, God is conceived as just, compassionate, forgiving—so much so that, as an act of infinite love, he sacrificed his only son on the cross of suffering to cleanse the sins of humankind and to reveal the path to salvation from the travails of earthly life and death. Love of God (*Agape*), then, is judged to be the true root from which love between persons ultimately springs. And what exactly is a higher human love? Perhaps being trusting, compassionate, and unselfish—that is, ideally to shoulder the burdens of others as if they are one's own—and to avoid seeing persons as just so many objects to be manipulated for one's own benefit.

Christian spiritual love, then, stands opposed to Freud's idea that love is inordinately egocentric, affirming instead that love is genuine only when it is compassionate and selfless—for it is only through these that loving fusion with others and with God is possible, signaling a movement of the soul toward moral-spiritual perfection. Above all, altruism and compassion must always be sincere, never used as masks to disguise shrewd calculations to manipulate others to gain pleasure and power at their expense. At issue here is whether the fusion experience inherent in both erotic and spiritual love is a selfish or selfless act, or some subtle blend of the two.

What is meant by fusion? It is an experience of surrender in a sensual or spiritual coupling of beings that heightens the senses and emotions to such intensity that the ordinary boundaries of the self are shattered. It is also found in the more gentle empathetic act of identifying with someone else so fully that one's sense of "I" melts away by being partially absorbed in the other. Whether driven by altruism or egotism, erotic and spiritual fusion share a common trait, namely, a drive to cross over the ordinary limits of self-identity into another sphere where one fuses with something greater than oneself (be it God, a person, or the forces of nature). Perhaps it is judicious to claim that the essence of love, despite its several varieties and objects, is an experience of self-transcendence that redeems the self from its ontological separation through a feeling of deep unity that appears at extraordinary moments in the course of living.

Whether the object of love is another's body, communion with God, or identification with a friend who is suffering, there is clearly a powerful human wish to dismantle sufficiently the protective walls of self-reference to be vulnerable to an experience of union. Perhaps the drive to achieve self-loss shares certain traits with dying—the sense that the "I" is draining away, losing control to an inexorable commanding power, and a foreboding feeling of annihilation. Both sensual and spiritual union are linked to death because it signifies the absolute return to unconsciousness, that is, to the not-self from which every living being arises and returns.

——— • • • ———

The universal yearning for love is paradoxically a desire for one's own death as an isolated being, bounded by both its body and the empirical realities of its everydayness. When the love-drive is considered from the perspective of fragile, pained, and needy creatures such as ourselves, it seems to offer at least a momentary feeling of redemption from the struggle, frustration, and aloneness that individuation naturally entails. But unlike the actual condition of death, the moment of loving is, strangely, a dying that fills the self with fullness and joy, for one has felt a transcendence born of self-loss.

It seems, then, that love in both the Freudian and Christian senses poses the paradox of offering great reward and severe risk: great reward because loving signifies the joyful sharing of body, spirit, or both that unshackles the self from its "prison" of existential isolation to experience that lovely forgetfulness that fusion brings; but also severe risk, because love's intimacy engenders a trusting, unprotected condition of spirit where the love-object—whether another person, God, or nature— is potentially positioned to exploit one's vulnerabilities, indeed, even to annihilate. That is why the person "in love" is always subject to deeper pain than the person who is being asked for love but fails to give it.

Still, when two mysteriously become one in an intense experience of unity, the everyday dualities between subject and object, the corporeal and spiritual, and self and other—from which our normal experience of separateness arises—melts away in a glorious transcendence. Alas, these sublime moments when eternity is deeply felt are inevitably followed by falling into the aloneness that is the fate of mortal beings. Descending from love's glory without our consent to the prison of self, and proceeding to peer at life and people with wary eyes as the world's anxieties, pressures, and duties clamor for attention, we can only hope that love's mystery will return to bequeath life's greatest treasure.

Memory

Fervent honesty toward oneself is necessary to exhume one's spiritual maladies and demons from secret recesses into mind's conscious light. After a lengthy period of judicious sifting and cleansing, these demons may finally be disbarred from inflicting further harm, at least after being finally banished to the sepulcher they deserve. Restoration to robust health—and everyone knows just how needed that is!—entails undergoing intense *anamnesis*; for without retrieving the past, the spirit cannot trace the subterranean paths through which anxiety and doubt came to shadow its experience of the present. Lacking such insight, spirit is sentenced to carry an even greater burden of suffering into the future.

The padlock that enchains memory in repressed forgetfulness can only be opened with the key of focused introspection; and failing that act of judicious reminder of all that one was—blindly loving, embracing wisely, hating unjustly, foolishly expecting, missing opportunities, fearing to explore mysteriously beckoning paths, hurting those we love, not returning love to those who freely offer it—the sullen shadows inside the fortress of self must grow increasingly restless and angry from neglect, until they finally rebel and escape their prison of repression to wreak revenge—whether as sweat-inducing nightmares that disturb restful sleep, as discomforting images and feelings that obsessively interrupt daylight life, or as frequent visits to an expensive psychoanalyst because one is insufferable to oneself and perhaps to others as well.

Memory, then, brings into acute awareness fragments of self-identity that, from rejection, neglect, embarrassment, or fright, grew stern and resentful at having little or no opportunity to argue their cases with all the vividness and emotional strength they could muster. After all, they are not only parts of oneself but make oneself *possible*, for things that are pushed into hidden realms continue to exert subtle effects.

Self-love is the essential step required to reconcile with oneself. The courage to recognize, and then embrace, all the diverse parts of what one was, even if these be dark, painful, and downright inconsistent, requires a capacity for self-love. The self is an intricate tapestry of threads woven from its unique past. Lacking discernment into the process by which we came to be what we are, we can neither understand the whole fabric of our being nor visualize the steps we must take as we climb the ladder into the future.

Walking Near the Abyss

At still moments, away from the noise and haste of everyday life that obscures me to myself, I seem to discern a difference between myself and others—namely, my willingness to admit freely what most appear to hide. Perhaps what sets me apart is my marked inability to disguise my pain and unclarity about existence behind pleasant social masks and civilities, although it would be vain to imply that I possess greater doses of courage and honesty than most. Is it possible that I might be an entirely self-indulgent individual who wears his heart on his sleeve for all to see because of a failure to ripen from immaturity into a prudent adult who has mastered the art of disguise as a condition of survival?

Leaving aside that possibility, I also notice that my eagerness to voice questions and doubts, indeed, to unveil my spirit for inspection, is what endears me to a special few, whereas most shrink back out of embarrassment or anxiety at my displays. Wishing to engage in serious, heartfelt sharing of my intellectual and moral uncertainties, I notice that most people decline my invitation to aid me in my perpetual struggle to achieve greater clarity, and that sometimes my presence may lead them to beat a hasty retreat to their safe cocoons.

Feeling perplexity and distrust at withdrawal from my overtures, I sometimes become angry and judge the mass of humanity—leaving aside the rare exception—to be rather cowardly, because they go to great lengths to insulate themselves from feeling the pain that honest self-reflection entails, weaving illusions of comfort and security to avoid recognizing that their lives are inherently obscure and ephemeral.

On those occasions when people strike me as especially distant and distrustful, and when the struggle for survival feels more a burden than a joy in a world filled with hardship, misunderstanding, and mutual abuse, I admit that life's tapestry weaves threads of doom as we roll along towards death. Hence, my impulse grows stronger to withdraw into that special place in myself that is free of social masks, material worries, and duties, to where secret feelings, thoughts, and yearnings silence my doubts to carry me gently along on kindly sea-currents to new and wonderful continents with vast interiors to explore. But sometimes I feel akin to a passenger on a tiny ship sailing along under the canopy of a darkened, windy sky that intimates the birth of an especially mighty hurricane, causing me to feel a terrifying foreboding that strips away my composure and teaches me just how powerless I am.

Life walks on a sunlit path strewn with tall brown trees, colorful flowers, and pungent aromas, and encircling this path is a great abyss into which life falls when losing its footing. True, there are many wondrous sites to behold as we stroll along, whether these be beautiful or ugly, peaceful or jarring, fulfilling or depleting, or joyful or melancholic. And yet one thing is utterly certain: life's perplexities and richness are vastly heightened by stopping now and then to gaze into that terrible abyss that eternally confronts us as we dangle precariously near it. Only then can we truly say we lived.

Realizing that I exist at the edge of an abyss which marks the point where life crosses over to death leads me to scribble compulsively and then to step back to ponder my own words. Meeting death without truly dying gives vision greater acuity, deepens perplexity, and is the origin of all earnest philosophizing. If my words are mere surface scratchings, and confused images of a sphere beyond linguistic representation, then perhaps it would be best to stop writing and listen to the silence—a pregnant silence filled with meaning, not the silence of emptiness. Sometimes my thoughts exhaust me, and I wish these volcanic eruptions of images and thoughts that well up from my being would cease, if only for a moment or two, so that my spirit can experience that healing rest that both calms and readies it for the next inevitable upheaval.

MOODS

Walking in Step with Life

Past and future enfold in mind's immediacy. No befores or afters but only nows. The perfected life of the timeless gods is beyond sight's horizon. Blemished and bewildered, we seek escape from life's confusing embrace. Still, banish the suspicion that life is a grimacing demon that enjoys inflicting pain and death on its offspring.

Walk in step with life, never before or after it, and learn to embrace it as I know you can. Drink its draughts and dance its dance, always tying the knot that binds joy and pain.

Let the spirit become flesh that touches another. Let the eye contemplate that radiant light that shines through us. Let love give joy without fear when it is time. Let the treacherous currents of life have their awesome swells and fearsome mysteries that silence noisy vanity. Embrace the moods that command. Resistance is futile, for you are a rolling wave on a boundless, turbulent sea waiting to scatter into the nameless when fate decrees.

Spirit

Silently and calmly, Spirit feels life's holy elixir flowing through its body-case of exquisitely carved channels. Enchained to Time's unbreakable cycle of death seeding birth and birth spawning death, Spirit beholds itself as a majestic tapestry of nameless weavings.

Best is that enigmatic silence that listens to leaves swaying on thorn-adorned trees standing high above a swiftly flowing river crowned by blue-tipped waves that crash relentlessly against magnificent unyielding boulders. See in the river's rush the eternal spawning of new forms decreed by the impenetrable will of a nameless Master-power. As the old passes into memory, and as the new takes hold, parched mouths drain delicious nectar from gilded cups to praise the power that births its children into daylight to seek their destinies.

Where We Dwell

As dew-laden skies trace a vast arc above where we dwell, and as Earth, the time-aged, spins on its pivot traversing the fiery sun, light-beams radiating from the daystar's molten center penetrate the formless darkness to display images of life. The fearless sage discerns that life is a step to death, death a step to life, and that life, death, and step are one, children of that resplendent source from where all beings emerge and return in the circle of circles.

Time's Duration

The woeful self is birthed and expires in Time's duration, opposing its puny will to winged Becoming while dwelling dark to itself in a prison-world, unaware of its true root. Oblivious to the power that fills great and small life with movement, color, and shape, the deluded self knows not it walks on paths decreed by invincible necessity. Enveloped in confusion and shorn from its ground, the self is lost to itself as it perishes in forgetfulness.

Exuberant Life

The eternal spring of life is love's blessedness which alone unbinds Spirit ensnared in heavy corporeal chains. Break the fetters of distress to seek the abode of exuberant life!

Become a hallowed ear attuned to the hushed tones of Wisdom's counsel: "Be aware of what is close at hand, whether dim figures sharing intimacies on a partially lit night, or haunting reveries that fill the soul with fearsome shades and sounds of terror. Observe the sun's noonday glowing warmth enfolding the Earth in bounteous glory. Then behold the countenance of the divine in things great and small as you listen to the voice that sweetly sings a glorious song of life and a solemn dirge of death."

Wild Desires

Wild desires howl victory, clawing a path with ragged talon and cruel tooth from gloomy prison into blinding day far beyond where Hades' jailer stood futile guard with key, whip, and chain. Obscene urges transmute into ominous silhouettes visible in space and time at mind's edge, craving retribution for eons of dismal oblivion.

Wild desires offer a gilded cup of nectar's sweet delight to ecstasy-craving lips as body is flooded by insatiable urges. Brittle reason shatters in sighs of holy frenzy. Siren-songs consecrate the spirit of earth as body disrobes to receive luxuriant warmth in rapturous embrace to seed the cadence of new life.

Destiny

Mortal eyes yearn to attain vision that penetrates the shrouded will of the Power that drives destiny. To behold the countenance of the boundless source that births the living as fragments of itself, wise spirits shed terrestrial eyes to flee from the incessant play of motley shapes that fleetingly and confusedly stream forth. Heed the heart's voice that hushedly reveals the hidden path to the greatest treasure. Destiny is prepared; silence marks the way; and surrender to the nameless one is not loss but resurrection from blindness to discernment.

The Lovers

A man and woman gaze through trembling light and dark shadows cast by candlelight, striving to glimpse the enticingly veiled being of the other. Soft, vulnerable eyes are filled with love's yearnings. Silence is not dark oblivion but restful prelude to the enchanted play of frenzied satyr and wreathed nymph, offspring of elusive Proteus, the disc-eyed.

For them, the moment banishes Time, the merciless God of gods, who wills that everything must perish in the restless cycle of beginnings and endings.

Time's grim duration is forgotten in the white heat of love's passion, alternating joy and tears in fleet succession as two beings become one. Eyes touching and melting, the corporeal and spiritual merge in a speechless instant of warmth and trust. Away dark shadows! Away angry Time that brings death as penalty to the living!

The spirit's emptiness is filled with life and unspeakable gratitude, for a lost Eternity is resurrected in the shining other, and love builds shared monuments to itself when glorious beams of boundless light descend on it as the wedding gift of the divine.

Sorrow

O sorrowful spirit enmeshed in the spider's web of your own creative weaving, hear my well-chosen words!

Let your flowing tears of regret be a treasure of white pearls that purify the spirit for new life. Savor the hallowed elixir that sates in joy and strength a gnawing spiritual thirst. Beam a lovely smile as winged vision pierces the darkness to where healing light dwells. Celebrate in wise silence as you behold the face of the limitless that dispels the cloak of paradox to join what seems severed. And know that you spawn new beginnings as the old passes into the shrine of memory and the present serves up refreshing, life-filling nectars.

Daybreak

Laden with daybreak's keen scent of moist earth, which arouses my spirit to tarry in the world of light, I yearn to find the secret source of the fragrance-call that awakens me to life. As misty dreams fade and day-passions stir, I hear the agitated calls of long-winged crested birds soaring high above the tallest sequoia trees—but far below somber gray-tinged clouds weighted with moisture-beads that fall as raindrops over where I stand.

Limber arms stretch forth as my fingers grope to touch the material source of that elusive earth-aroma that caresses my very core. Still, I know not where to turn, for the scent is both far and near, having equal power everywhere. Ensnared by the earth's fragrance that beckons me, I eagerly seek its origin, as if the spiritual and corporeal must merge in its blessed presence.

Reason tells me its source is near, for it, like everything existent, is visible in a definite space and time. What *Is* cannot be if nowhere! As I roam about my little world, finding no trustworthy path to the place sought, I conclude on this glorious sunlit day that the earth-aroma belongs neither to a here nor a there. It is that blessed daybreak when the spirit finds the center everywhere to behold in the god's fragrance that awakens life.

Rapture

A gateway to grace is unveiled in your rapturous caress. The abyss that divides worlds is bridged by your flashing hazel eyes, olive-hued delicate skin, and golden curls that sparkle glory. Desire grows into raging flames that burn away the cheerless malaise of two lonely spirits.

O, the promise of grace turns to sorrow as measureless passions flare and pain consumes us. We unwittingly serve the evil designs of cruel divinities descending from secret spheres to thwart our soul-lights from attaining the brighter glow of the two become one. False hopes weave a tapestry of illusion, and time's mutation dashes promise of union as the trickster gods laugh mightily at our deepening grief. The glimpse of eternity is washed away in a tide of melancholic tears.

Dawn

Weary eyes sluggishly open as night dreams yield to Dawn's merciless assault. Inward vision disperses as radiant sunlight envelops me in colors, sounds, and shapes that clamor for attention. I dwell in that open space where sight sees things chained to space and time. Dispelled are vivid night dreams of our boundless, fertile mother who brings forth her children into life to tarry as sufferers. Being merciful, she always recalls her progeny to the womb where hardship and division are vanquished.

You

Thinking about *you* is like the dance of light cast by flickering candles on a moonlit night, or like the perpetual play of whitish waves on a swiftly flowing river at sunset. Silently feeling *you* dispels the darkness as the soul's vision penetrates the house of Being to illuminate its countless rooms.

Alas, words are insolent vanities and empty sound compared to *you*, for your terrain is strewn with hieroglyphs only the initiate may, with your succor, hope to decipher.

You don an abundance of opaque garments that you hesitate to bare, even to your initiate; and yet you slyly invite the eye to pierce your semblance to behold the exquisite nakedness beyond. *You* whisper secrets to me, your loving disciple, that illuminate your being and becoming, and, as true supplicant, I partake of the joy and grief of your sacred polarity.

Signs

Signs to behold:

In the shallow, strained breath of a dying man
    resting on bone-white hospital sheets.
In pale blue eyes encircled by unresting
    bronze lids of fluttering skin.
In the suicide flight of a speckled yellow moth
    into the alluring hot flame.
In green vegetation turning charred-brown on a
    balmy summer day.
In the caressing mouths of gentle lovers
    in their favorite city park by the lake.
In life's colorful play of dark and light moods
    that change without asking.
In the dream-castles of night where
    well-furnished rooms abound to be discovered.
In the tender feelings that bloom
    into the sweetest of kisses and hopes.
And in the imagining of distant worlds floating in
    boundless spaces between Alpha and Omega.

Life

Life: seeking the greatest joy in crossing craggy ravines to ascend the peaks of mighty mountains that touch the sky; strolling pleasantly and securely along flat plains where no threatening shadow is concealed to vision; feeling the incessant play of dark and light moods that sway the spirit from holy calm to restless foreboding and to every imaginable state between; and setting forth on unknown seas to find new treasures in faraway lands that beckon to us in prescient dreams.

Spider's Web

Why do I fear death? Is it because I feel its uncanny shadow-presence in the swirl of somber thoughts that haunt me without relief except in rare moments of darkened, dreamless sleep? Am I the living puppet of some sadistic master-creator who bore me only to enjoy pulling the strings of my life's dance? Why do I write? Can words touch others through the eye when my voice fails to sound in their ears?

Am I evil, the carrier of a poisonous black dust that invisibly seeds the air that others breathe, causing their lungs to sprout plants of death? Are my words incomprehensible? Can we truly fathom each other, or are we walled into silent prisons despite the illusion that gesture, sound, and sight bridge the measureless, chilly spaces between minds and bodies?

Perhaps I am a human spider weaving a web-house where I dwell in fear that the silken filaments will rip apart from the swaying motions I unleash as I move about my little world. Should I fully embrace all the contradictions of my being, suffer through their struggles, and acknowledge the exhaustion that follows to be a holy weariness born of satiety in life's incessant play?

Am I the battlefield where unknown selves vie for power to fashion my conscious identity according to their own likeness, each seeking to be the exclusive ruler of mind and body? Indeed, can my words be trusted and coherent if my "I" is really composed of many layers that, when peeled away, always reveal more ones to behold—*ad infinitum*?

KNOWING

A Report to the Children of the Planet Athanatos on the State of Wisdom Among Earthlings

My dearest, most loving children: I was recently appointed by the distinguished members of the ruling High Commission of our planet Athanatos to visit Earth to observe the moral and spiritual condition of the human species. As you know, Athanatos circles the twin-stars we call Philosophia and Kallos every hundred earth-years and is located in the Orphic galaxy that is one million two thousand light-years from Earth, which according to our precise calculations, will evaporate in a blaze of molten fury in four billion three hundred thousand years and six days from today when the sun of its solar system explodes in a glorious supernova.

The inhabitants of all the worlds originate from the Demiurge's eternal embryo, who felt great joy in conceiving its progeny and endowing them with its seed of eternal wisdom as their supreme birthright. It is the Demiurge's plan for its children to cultivate that seed into a beautiful blossoming flower that signals the attainment of unity and perfection. As it stands, humans are a rather lowly and bewildered life-form when viewed against the backdrop of the many highly evolved beings that populate the countless planets scattered throughout the vast expanse of galaxies in space and time.

We perfected, deathless beings of the planet Athanatos intend to invite the Earthlings—several million years from today—to depart their isolated planet, long before its destruction, to meet their brethren on other worlds in a spirit of love, communion, and peace. For that sublime event to occur, humans must mature the germs of philosophical wisdom which currently lie dormant in their nature. Without tending the plant of wisdom, they will neither be able to dispel the barbarism, confusion, and ignorance that ensnares them, nor journey to where they will joyfully behold the beautiful countenance of the Demiurge—the eternal spring from which goodness and salvation flows. They as yet fail to understand that it was from an experience of divine loneliness that the Demiurge fashioned living beings with whom to share its delight in creation. Indeed, the Demiurge filled them with a longing to become whole, and lovingly bequeathed to them fragments of its eternal light to illuminate the path that leads to abiding happiness.

The visits of Athanatosians to backward planets such as Earth are absolutely undetectable to their inhabitants, because we long ago shed our bodily prisons to become a purely spiritual life-form that exists outside the spatial, temporal, and causal laws that make human cognition possible. Leaving not the slightest trace of our presence, we freely and invisibly move about the many populated worlds to carry out our mission of gathering information about their progress in attaining divine wisdom. Remaining invisible is essential, given the Demiurge's injunction against highly developed beings having any contact with relatively primitive and violence-prone species.

Although we perfected ones feel compassion for the suffering that humans inflict on their own kind, and eternal love for a race that carries in themselves the image of the Demiurge, we know that intervening in their affairs to stop their violence and heal their pain—and to teach them the ultimate mysteries of life and death—would be absolutely futile. Indeed, they cannot see or hear of things for which they lack vision and hearing at their current stage of development.

It took millions of earth years for us Athanatosians to open the seals of wisdom to behold her glories. That journey required painful struggle, self-reflection, and self-discipline to abolish from ourselves every trace of jealousy, vanity, stupidity, violence, competition, and hatred. These unhappy traits—which frequently mark the conduct of humans on the planet Earth—were wisely woven into the material garment of all primitive beings by the Demiurge. Dwelling in finite body-garments subject to decay and death causes backward creatures like the Earthlings to experience terrible anxiety, confusion, and loneliness, from which arises a deep thirst for insight into the reasons for their unhappy condition.

Spirits encased in matter inevitably view life from the standpoint of their self-regarding, individualized egos. But their condition of being separated creatures is not the whole story, for the Demiurge fashioned them to have physical and emotional needs for survival, reproduction, companionship, and love that can only be met by forging dependent relationships with other living beings. Humans, then, are naturally self-protective because they dread the loss of autonomy that signals vulnerability to being controlled by others; and yet they are also compelled to relinquish their defensive egos to fulfill themselves by compassionately identifying with the hardships of others. Indeed, they waver between the poles of attraction and repulsion—attraction being an impulse toward unity and love, whereas repulsion is essential for maintaining the boundary of individuation.

Humans often display the traits of extreme selfishness, ruthless competitiveness, and lust for power when they compete to assimilate nutrients from the natural world, when they are moved to sexually embrace to procreate the next generation, and when they seek out friendships to quell their loneliness. Failing to harmonize their individual needs and wills, they manifest a negative spirit that causes the mutual infliction of harm. They lack the wisdom to see that the ephemeral victories gained by egotism, violence, power-seeking, and manipulation can neither fill their emptiness with true substance nor protect them against aging and death.

The Demiurge's plan for the education and evolution of humans requires that they waver between the contradictory poles of attraction and repulsion.

That wavering produces extremes of joy and suffering, love and hate, altruism and egotism, beauty and ugliness, and peace and violence. Severe imbalances of spirit are the root of their propensity to do both evil and good. Over time they will see that negativity engenders futility, misery, and vanity, and that these lead them nowhere but to the abyss. If virtue, temperance, and love are to be inscribed in the human spirit—and not habitually espoused as hypocritical rhetoric belied by conduct—then the deformity of evil must be overcome in their spirits. Indeed, the Earthlings must tread an arduous path before they can fully perceive the light of the Demiurge that alone teaches them how to harmonize—and finally transcend—their natural polarities.

———   •••   ———

There exist two basic varieties of knowledge-seekers among the Earthlings: first, the numerous academic researchers and teachers that congregate in institutions of higher learning; and second, the tiny group of genuine philosophers that impart original insights that long outlive the rise and fall of fickle intellectual fashion.

These two types of knowledge-seekers are marked by distinct mental and imaginative capacities, divergent senses of vocation, and different views of the nature and goals of knowledge. Although some hybrids exist who incorporate traits of both academics and philosophers—like an alloy of impure metals or a mixture of incompatible emotions—my observations are limited to disclosing the essential qualities of the two generic types. Further, as we Athanatosians love melodies that fill our beings with the divine harmonies of the Demiurge that resound through the whole of creation, I will often employ musical imagery to show how the impulses, judgments, and concepts of academics and philosophers resonate different tones in the spirits of their listeners.

Academic word-compositions are rather abstract, formal, and prolix; they usually sound dry, repetitive, and earthbound to the listener. Indeed, music that originates solely in the intellectual faculty—isolated from the deep reservoirs of intuition and feeling—lacks the necessary imaginative vision and expressive power to help the Earthlings open their hearts and eyes to receive insights that transfigure their spirits.

We Athanatosians learned from eons of education in the hard school of material existence that the ability to embrace contraries—joy and pain, unity and division, conflict and cooperation, clarity and paradox, and good and evil—is essential for the deepening of wisdom. Life is akin to a music that sounds great contrasts, from dissonances that evoke terror and despair to pleasing chords that calm and balance the spirit. Sadly, the academic mind reacts unfavorably to the presence of intellectual uncertainty and excessive emotion. Driven to impose order when confronted by paradox and ambiguity, the academic often pursues a type of knowledge that skims surfaces and avoids the depths, preferring to classify facts and events into abstract schemes that hardly do justice to the inherent richness of life. Too often, academic knowledge is akin to music that is monotonous, flat-sounding, and composed of familiar tunes and tame harmonies.

As a result, academic compositions rarely wrestle with, or cast much light on, the great questions posed by human existence, be these about good and evil, truth and illusion, freedom and authority, body and spirit, or death and immortality. Lacking attunement to the Demiurge's harmonious order of being from which wisdom's glory eternally springs, academics are largely unable to serve as exemplary teachers to the many Earthlings who are floundering in ignorance and confusion.

When observing the behavior of academic knowledge-seekers, I noticed frequent displays of an annoying trait of bloated self-importance. In a word, vanity. They act as if the Demiurge specially chose them to occupy the highest rung on the ladder of being to serve as ideal specimens of humanity. Naturally, I also felt dismay when seeing their strong inclination to be petty, gossipy, and denigrating of rival colleagues. Indeed, they frequently lack the divine virtue of humility. Humility is absolutely essential for cultivating the highest degree of philosophical wonder in the face of life's mysteries, for listening in silent attentiveness to the sublime music inscribed in every soul by the Demiurge, and for feeling the presence of that noble spiritual thirst that alone is sated at wisdom's golden well.

My dear Athanatosian children, I expect you will share my disappointment at observing the inclination of academics to believe that their dim flickers of mind-light are akin to bright suns that radiate insights of world-historical importance. They will never know that we—the perfected offspring of the Demiurge—are hardly impressed by their strutting about as peacocks! Still, my critical remarks about academics should be balanced by the knowledge that the Demiurge's plan is to perfect his human offspring in the fullness of time.

We must patiently await the passage of many eons for the academics to see that their dwelling in musty, book-lined caves leads them to confound their elementary thoughts with the glorious rays of eternal truth. The time will arrive when their thinking transmutes into raging flames of insight that burn away every impurity of intellect, feeling, and spirit. Then they will experience a sacred dawn that signals the birth of an insatiable desire to depart their caves to touch the colorful blossoms of abundant life germinating outside in the rich soil. Only then will they be able to decipher the hieroglyphs of the Demiurge's evolutionary plan.

— ••• —

Scattered like rare diamonds among the humans are a few philosophers who escaped the caves of ignorance and vanity to direct their sight to where the eternal sunlight of truth illuminates the face of the

Demiurge. Their well-chosen, sculptured words—like beautiful symphonies and delicate chamber works wrought by master composers—elevate and harmonize the emotions, open the mind's eye to new realms of meaning, and dispel the cloudy veils of ignorance that prevent humans from seeing themselves as microcosms of the Demiurge's macrocosm. Despite their rarity, the thought-seeds of philosophers will eventually take root to blossom into splendid plants of wisdom to sate the growing hunger of humans to know from where they originated, to where they have arrived, and to where they must go after death. Then will despair, confusion, and violence be forever banished.

The few philosophers who embody humanity's highest hope currently suffer a terrible lot as they struggle to find ears to listen to their sublime music—indeed, a music that is often drowned out by the noisy siren songs of the academic pedagogues, who seduce the many into believing that they alone possess wisdom. To make matters worse, the small number of philosophical spirits are often treated as heretics deserving of silence or persecution by defenders of religious and intellectual fashion. True philosophers evoke envy in narrow-minded, insecure spirits for manifesting purity of heart and intellect, and for their uncompromising efforts to raise humans from ignorance, error, and violence to a vision of themselves as the offspring of the Demiurge, who gave them the gift of life for the sole purpose of learning how to love. Love alone redeems the tormented spirit from isolation, anxiety, and despair, and love's promise of unity is only realized when self-will and selfishness are extinguished from the spirit.

The conflict between philosophers and false teachers of wisdom is hardly new in human history. We Athanatosians witnessed how Heraclitus, Empedocles, Socrates, and Plato struggled mightily against the Homeric bards and sophists for spreading harmful beliefs about morality and the godhead, and for teaching the aristocratic youth of Athens that mastering the art of rhetoric is superior to truth-seeking. How tragic that Socrates was put to death for voicing the noble sentiment that caring for one's soul takes infinite precedence over seeking political power, wealth, and worldly success. Throughout history the few truly inspired philosophers rightly taught that virtue and abiding happiness spring from self-knowledge—indeed, that self-knowledge alone unlocks the secret door that leads the spirit to commune with the Demiurge's order of being.

On previous visits we sadly observed that other great teachers of wisdom, whether Confucius, Jesus, Buddha, Seneca, Plotinus, Spinoza, Böhme, Eckhart, Nietzsche, or Schopenhauer, to name just a few—were targeted for persecution by the sophists of their day for teaching ideas they considered mortal threats to their own. Still, we Athanatosians recognize that strife, sacrifice, and error must exist in order for wisdom to evolve; and knowing that, we feel joy that seeded among the humans are a few philosophers who devote their lives to igniting in others that holy desire to remove every stupidity, insensitivity, jealousy, and vanity that perverts their spirits.

Of late the sophists are acutely aware that they are failing in their cunning designs to persuade people that they alone are the true repositories of wisdom. To prevent being unmasked, they utilize the latest technologies—radio, television, e-mail, Internet, and the mass publication of magazines, periodicals, and books—to propagate their fashionable ideas. Indeed, some academics confuse people hungry for wisdom by giving off the false impression that they alone should be relied on for authoritative insights into seminal philosophical works by virtue of possessing advanced educational degrees.

These self-appointed academic popularizers of great ideas and traditions produce a flood of books, essays, and articles that disseminate their interpretations of philosophers for mass consumption, and they are often applauded by people who falsely think themselves lacking in sufficient specialized education to appreciate works of genius. It is rather ironic that the seminal philosophers usually express their rich insights in writing styles that are direct, simple, powerful, and fully accessible to any intelligent individual motivated to struggle to find wisdom. Unfortunately, academic scribbling is often incomprehensible to persons lacking specialized vocabulary, and gives the false impression that there is gold to be found buried in those jargon-laden words.

Great ideas are treated by these academic sophists as tasty morsels of food to be gobbled down without fully savoring their subtle flavors, showing they lack real respect for the philosophical chefs who struggled mightily to concoct nourishing dishes for persons needful of wisdom. Every Athanatosian is mortified to behold the miserable treatment inflicted on the philosophers' offspring—their thoughts—by the sophists who fail to appreciate the loving and arduous labor required to bring these golden children into the light of day.

The goal of transmuting great philosophical concepts into fashionable discourse to further academic advancement and prestige easily fosters selective, one-sided explications of seminal ideas. Sympathetically explaining the ideas that please them while criticizing the ones they decide are defective, many academics fail to recognize that original philosophies must be grasped as a whole before the individual parts can be properly understood. After all, engaging in earnest dialogue with great philosophers is quite unlike cracking nuts. If the sophists succeeded in fully digesting the wholesome foods of philosophers, then they would no longer suffer from bouts of mental indigestion, and perhaps they would also cure themselves of the tunnel vision that prevents sight from soaring to heights where things are perceived in their essential, enduring outlines. More often the sophists orbit as planets around the radiant sun of philosophy, capable only of reflecting light and never generating their own brightness.

So ends my report to the children of the planet Athanatos.

Halls of Academe

No person is exempt from feeling that special heaviness of spirit that arises from recognizing that life failed in essential respects to turn out as hoped, be this due to missed opportunities for love and friendship, for career advancement, or for greater material security and spiritual growth. Sensing defeat in the present, and lamenting past mistakes, we may fashion a prison-house of regrets that is not easily escaped. Radical honesty and a strong dose of courage are needed to admit the unsettling truth that some of our core values and activities forge strong chains that hinder life. From that awareness may arise the will to shatter the chains so that new, free, and creative selves emerge from our smothering tangle of self-inflicted fears, unproductive habits, and ill-chosen duties. And it is probably true that many fail to escape their prison-houses because they do not heed the voice within that issues a call to change life's course before the advent of death makes that impossible.

For me, writing *At the Edge of the Abyss* was an act of shedding a disquieting academic *persona* to enable my spirit's true music to find audible expression. Finally ceasing to visualize myself as a full-fledged member of the clan of academic philosophers, I no longer desired to write specialized, jargon-filled articles and books armed with massive amounts of quotations and footnotes to justify claims that meant little to anyone except a very small group of professional intellectuals. In the Halls of Academe I felt like a confused elephant living in the cold wastes of the Antarctic searching for green vegetation to sate its hunger—and also for a tree to rub against to relieve an unrelenting itch.

Academic intellectuals—especially the professional philosophers and political theorists with whom I am most acquainted—often claim that the true value of Ivory Tower life is the protection it offers against outside pressures—be these governments, corporations, or interest groups, that threaten the ability to teach freely and to seek knowledge. Thinking that they possess a nobler calling than found in the pursuits of less formally educated persons, academics often smugly judge them to be rather uncultured and ignorant—mistakenly believing that specialized, advanced education guarantees the learning of wisdom.

Despite this self-lauding rhetoric, academic intellectuals fiercely compete for professional advancement, power, and reputation, a fact that belies their claim to be more judicious and independent than persons employed directly in the trades and professions of the market economy, who also struggle to harvest the fruits of their labor. In short, academic intellectuals, like all hired workers, remain utterly dependent on their institutions and powerful colleagues for income, security, and status, and hence are subject to pressures to behave in ways that often contradict their idealistic rhetoric.

While maintaining the dignified facade of the academic life and its noble values, many institutional intellectuals hasten to conceal their "human, all too human" traits (to borrow a phrase from Nietzsche): competitiveness, jealousy, fear, vanity, and ambition for power and prestige. Younger academics are especially vulnerable to these vices. Anxious for their future, overly sensitive to criticism of their work, and utterly dependent on senior faculty for advancement and tenure, many learn to cultivate an excessive prudence—at the cost of their intellectual and moral integrity. Eventually, they find themselves restricting their own research and writing, lest they stray into dangerous territory unsanctified by the established canons—or fashions—of their scholarly fields.

Courage, creative imagination, and genuine insight are rare and precious qualities among thinkers and educators in any age. It is the unfortunate rule in almost every historical period that many institutional intellectuals are seduced by promises of material gain, professional status, and job security to conform to the agendas of governments, churches, the wealthy, and influential disseminators of current fashion. Thinking motivated by genuine perplexity, integrity, and love of truth can be the occasion for its practitioner to be shunned or punished for challenging conventional ideas and practices. When philosophizing is tethered to calculations of prudence and material advantage, it cannot spread its wings and soar to where thought may penetrate through dark clouds to visualize life in its bold outlines and to weigh the true value of existence.

— ••• —

The frequent displays of backbiting, fawning, and pettiness that mark academic pursuits create an unhealthy soil for cultivating what Hannah Arendt called the "life of the mind." Except for the rare scholar of judicious character and imaginative power who also has a full heart and a genuine spirit of fairness, academic intellectuals tend to be insecure and contentious spirits who congregate in factions of the like-minded to reinforce their shared prejudices. Indeed, they spend much valuable time together gossiping abusively about disliked colleagues whom they rarely confront directly with their true feelings, preferring to hide these behind a mask of hypocritical civility.

A vice that often marks the institutional intellectual is a certain tunnel vision that springs from being overspecialized. Practitioners in a particular field of study, be it philosophy, history, political science, sociology, psychology or economics, find it difficult to dialogue with professionals in other fields—or even in subfields of their own discipline—because they usually inhabit distinct linguistic, conceptual, and methodological universes learned from years of advanced education.

That unfortunate situation currently typifies the practice of academic philosophy and, in my estimation, has led to a serious dissipation of the original Socratic impulse to address issues of common concern in a comprehensible language. We are witness to a steep decline of the ability of intellectuals to develop a penetrating and colorful view of life as a whole and to address issues of value and meaning that perplex people as they struggle to gain clarity about their uncertain lives.

Over time I lost the desire to participate in that strange academic alchemy of transmuting the great ideas of fertile, passionate, and enduring philosophical texts of genius into sanitized and often fashionable professional intellectual discourse. Indeed, I no longer visualized a life devoted to penning specialized critical commentaries—for professional journals that very few people read—on a pantheon of seminal thinkers whose teachings are evaluated through conceptual lenses provided by reigning if fickle academic fashion.

It finally struck me as a fruitless task to compete in the academic game of trying to gain professional applause for offering ingenious insights into what, for instance, Plato, Aristotle, Kant, Hegel, Schopenhauer, Nietzsche, Weber, Heidegger, or Arendt "*really* meant." Rather, we should savor having dialogues with the seminal texts of genius instead of relying upon secondary works that academics provide to interpret their ideas. Scholarly confusions, errors of judgment, and biases are easily accepted by their readers as the gospel truth, especially if the readers lack time and motivation to read and think deeply about great books in an effort to cultivate independent critical judgment and to broaden their field of vision.

To satiate our thirst for wisdom, it is best to begin by drinking at the pure and deep wells of original thinkers rather than from the small cups provided by academic specialists. How exhilarating to accept the challenge to judge the worth of our favorite values, ideas, and conducts in an earnest critical encounter with the philosophical, political, and ethical views of master-thinkers! Only after we arrive at our own interpretations and judgments will a judicious reading of a few notable secondary scholarly works have real value.

---   •••   ---

Academic intellectuals justify their claims and interpretations by recourse to commonly accepted standards of scholarly writing and evidence. Their articles and books are usually filled with a wealth of footnotes and large bibliographies that clearly imply that the authors' claims and interpretations are just because these arose from a mastery and a fair-minded sifting of the relevant secondary literature. Yet it is hardly a secret that most academic writing is frequently obscure both to the educated public and to other scholars who are unfamiliar with a particular field's specialized languages, concepts, and methods. Indeed, obscurity and complexity can be used by academics to create a facade of profundity where none actually exists, to intimidate the trusting reader into accepting their claims as "truth" by shielding themselves from critical scrutiny, and to persuade the reader to rely on authority of others as evidenced by a torrent of claims and footnotes.

The scholarly ideal of objectivity easily conceals the fact that an author's citations can be highly selective, that is, deliberately chosen to rationalize a host of ideological biases and personal agendas as "impartial" findings and trustworthy interpretations of evidence. Deliberate or semi-conscious masking of what actually occurs enables scholars to claim—often with a superior air—that the ideas and interpretations of rivals are hopelessly tainted by factual inaccuracies and unsound theoretical premises whereas their own views and evidence are eminently fair.

Something else of importance struck me about the reality of academic life. Many scholars begin their careers by disciplining themselves (to varying degrees) to leading master-academics from whom they learn a host of special theories, values, and methods which decisively form their intellectual identities. Sometimes they act as if their masters possessed the gospel truth and alone provided the sacred keys that unlocked the wisdom hidden in seminal texts. Seeing themselves as members of a master's circle, and feeling loyalty to other followers with whom they share common habits of mind and intellectual projects, the disciples often narrow their field of vision to the point of being incapable of independent critical dialogue either with original texts or with the arguments of other academics who offer serious challenges to their own views.

It is eminently forgivable that the great majority of academic intellectuals are hardly original thinkers. After all, the presence of genius in our midst is a rare and decidedly unexpected event in world history—perhaps akin to the infrequent appearance of comets that arrive from the far reaches of space to illuminate briefly the heavens as we watch in amazement.

Still, without the gift of genius it is most difficult to seed thoughts that grow into mature and tasty fruits that satiate minds hungry for insight—let alone to spark flames of knowledge that shine brightly across the rise and fall of generations to enter the treasure-house of human wisdom. Instead, what academic intellectuals generally offer today is an almost endless repetition of assumptions, concepts, and methods derived from culturally fashionable discourse, be it postmodernism, poststructuralism, New Age spirituality, feminism, or neo-Marxism.

Ideally, one must be a master to dialogue at the highest level with the rich and challenging spirits of truly seminal thinkers. That dialogue requires imagination, a passionate love of ideas, and a courageous will to truth that refuses to be broken by material hardship, distorted by intellectual fashion, or routed by ridicule. These qualities of personal character and vision are often the very ones lacking in the majority of academic philosophers, although it is just to admit that every human being is marked by some moral and intellectual defect, be it a professional thinker, a factory worker, or even a genius.

The few genuine masters, then, stand on mountain peaks high above the academic philosophers, who inhabit the valleys below surrounded by dense forests that partially dim the sun's radiance from reaching them in its full measure of illumination. You can dialogue with the masters' offspring—their thoughts!—whenever you pick up their books, and I counsel you to do just that instead of reading the great majority of their academic interpreters, who more often than not lead you into a maze of confusing complexities that rarely speak to the important issues of life. After all, rare diamonds are much more beautiful to behold than the dubious glitter of imitation stones.

Immediacy and Abstraction

Contemporary geneticists, biologists and neurologists optimistically follow scientific protocols in an effort to demystify states of feeling and conscious awareness by tracing these to physical causes—as if every emotional and cognitive condition must originate in the interplay of underlying chemical, electrical, genetic, and somatic processes. The spheres of thought, emotion, and spirit—traditionally the distinctive traits that separate humans from other life-forms—have lost their mystery much in the way that materialist oriented astronomers, physicists, and geologists currently visualize nature as a desacralized realm of brute facts and processes governed by theoretically discernible objective laws.

Materialist accounts of the causal variables presumed responsible for a variety of ideational and emotional states fail to do justice to the actual lived experiences of persons. Consciousness consists of a steady stream of feelings, perceptions, and thoughts that momentarily arise and fall in mind for reasons that, at bottom, are always imprecise and conjectural. Mental life, then, consists of a continuous series of integral subjective experiences whereas scientific investigations attempt to analyze these experiences in terms of underlying material processes. The claim that the contents of mental life are always the effects of physical, empirical causes rests on the dubious assumption that matter is primary and that states of mind always derive from various combinations of matter. The difficulty is that the great variety of mental and emotional experiences defies explanation in terms of precise physical causes.

For example, what aggregate of somatic, chemical, and genetic factors explains why I experience perplexity, anxiety, and even anger at visualizing myself to be an ephemeral being whose every breath, thought, and action are uncanny? And what exact material causes are at work when I ponder the meaning of the fact that the human species is composed of billions of individuals who appear and disappear in the perpetual cycle of life and death without spending much time wondering about the nature of the place to where they arrived or about what they ought to do with their brief time?

How is the devoted scientific materialist to explain my feeling despair at knowing myself to be akin to a drop of water that will evaporate on some unknown day when the sun burns furiously hot for me alone? Indeed, what are the causal forces that lead me to wonder why we—the progeny of a concealed ground of being—are fated to tarry briefly and often confusedly in the daylight before illness erodes our bodies and death restores us to the source from which we sprung? And why did that unknown ground of being desire to create a universe inhabited by creatures subject to the limiting forces of space, time, and causality? Can materialist science shed light on why I—and perhaps you!—belong to the chorus of voices that protest being thrown into a condition of pain for which our consent was not solicited?

If I am unpersuaded that scientific materialism can explain the precise causal reasons for the succession of emotions, images, and thoughts that flow through my consciousness—such as my feeling metaphysical wonder at the strangeness of human existence—then I must conclude that the course of my mental life is largely undetermined by causal forces external to itself. It is a fruitless endeavor trying to explain scientifically why I choose to spend my leisure time pondering life's paradoxes even while I recognize that gaining absolute clarity is perhaps an impossible task.

— ••• —

It seems that I have encountered no divine or human beings—be these enlightened gurus, scientific materialists, academic philosophers, or theologians—to teach me an unassailable wisdom to satisfy my perplexity, but only "human, all too human" individuals whose vanity often leads them to expect homage even while they issue specious claims to knowledge. Thrown back on myself to be guided by the candle-light of thought—and in communion with the challenging reflections of a few sublime predecessors who invited their readers to hold dialogue about things that matter to living—I seek to find my way out of the cave of ignorance to the sun of knowledge. For me, thinking is endless because clarity is not easily found in an ambiguous human condition that always transcends the categories we use to fathom its nature.

That is why I sometimes visualize my life as akin to standing at a bustling downtown corner of a great city watching the steady flow of people pass before me without gaining clear recognition of their individual features, since no one stops to talk with me, a perfect stranger. Still, I endeavor to search their fleeting, dim faces in the hope of learning a secret or two, and if fortune favors me on some fine, bright day, I might meet that special "someone" who stops, gently takes my hand, and guides me to where the blazing sun dispels the darkness. In truth, that special "someone" is none other than myself exercising the power of reflection.

— ••• —

Creative imagination is required to transform the incessant play of pre-linguistic perceptions and feelings into definite mental images and ideas. The mind actively legislates boundaries between inner and outer worlds, and fills each of these with distinct contents by shaping the plural stream of experiences into orderly objects and events that occupy space, have causal efficacy, and manifest temporal change. Thinking philosophically about the variety of life's paradoxes and problems always entails linguistic articulation of experiences that initially belong to a silent sphere that lies beyond the power of conceptual representation.

If the self that contemplates itself and the world is always partly estranged from its objects of reflection—at least in the sense that its concepts, judgments, and observations are never fully adequate to the momentary experiences that endlessly flow through it—then I am compelled to admit that the words before you, my reader, cannot fully capture the elusively effervescent realities that I retrospectively rendered from immediacy into abstraction.

Beware of philosophers and scientists who claim nearly absolute conceptual clarity by means of rigid schemes of definition, classification, and explanation. They succumb to the illusion that their abstract edifices are adequate renditions of an objective reality that they are privileged to know with relative certainty. That illusion breeds an insufferable vanity because of the failure to recognize that lifeless abstractions serve to coerce reality into distorted and rigid logical schemes.

Philosophers of enduring merit always possess a strong dose of poetic imagination. What cannot be rendered precisely in the abstract concept is best alluded to by a well-chosen evocative image, story, or myth that directly and powerfully resonates in the mind to bring to clear awareness what is already sensed in a pre-articulate way.

The deepest insights are best shared through

indirect utterances, such as when Plato poetically weaves the Allegory of the Cave to convey his mystical experience of touching a ground of wisdom that lay beyond the grasp of fickle sense-perception. Employing allegory to help his audience experience themselves and the cosmos anew, Plato asks that people remove the blinders that prevent sight from visualizing, however elusively, things that they already possess, for they could not possibly seek, or know, things that belong to an ontological sphere entirely separate from themselves.

Courage is needed to step outside the familiar shadowy caves of ignorance and common belief and journey with Socrates toward the Sun of wisdom. And although the traveler initially may seem to be engaged in a movement from a lower to a higher sphere of being, one is soon amazed to discover that what is found was already possessed by oneself. A knowing that matters is inseparable from self-recognition. Ascending is also descending into oneself.

Plato realized that if he tried to justify his philosophical claims—which often flew in the face of Athenian tradition and common belief—by sole recourse to abstract reasoning and logical proof, then the likely result would be for his audience to become resistant and even actively hostile. He decided that the articulation of his striking, unsettling ideas often required a mytho-poetic language to complement his formal arguments and proofs. In that way the normally separate domains of the abstract idea and intuitive insight would be bridged and made complementary.

But a serious dilemma arises. If the abstract concept fails to provide adequate distillations of lived experience, then it is also true that intuitive feeling faces a severe limitation despite its intrinsic richness—namely, that it is always imprisoned within an immediacy that is beyond direct linguistic representation. It is often difficult to get others precisely to comprehend one's own feelings and ideas even when stated with the greatest care. Frustration easily follows from a failure to find words that—no matter how well fashioned—seem to miss the mark both to ourselves and especially to others, whose facial expressions and speech belie their claim to "understand" the rich nuances of another's experience.

Complete sharing of the experiential worlds of persons is intrinsically difficult—and perhaps utterly impossible—and not just because humans have separate bodies and minds. It seems persons possess two different and often antithetical faculties of knowing, namely, reason and intuition.

Reason issues logical claims and arguments in the medium of language which, in principle, are susceptible to inspection, revision, and refutation by others. Further, rational propositions always transform sensuous, immediate experiences into ordered abstractions that are inexact condensations of reality. Intuition is a direct way of knowing that rests on prelinguistic states of feeling. As such, these states not only precede but defy exact identification and explanation. Reflecting on an experience involves imposing a conceptual category on the original one. Adherents of intuition reject efforts to identify and explain their direct experiences by means of precise conceptual schemes because these always seem to miss the mark.

It seems that to be a self is to have a mode of being that wavers between its reasoning and feeling faculties. Perhaps it is that constant wavering that gives human life its identity as a vagabond with no permanent resting place to call home.

Precipice of Knowledge

As we travel on life's familiar roads and obscure byways we are not wholly without maps to help us find our way. It is reasonable to ask exactly "who" designed the maps and "why?" It would be most consoling to believe that some powerful being, feeling pity at our condition of uncertainty and fear, decided to help us by bequeathing laws and precepts to direct our lives. Yet it is unlikely that the maps that guide our thought and action are the creative gifts of either a beneficent divinity or a wise human legislator. There is little reason to assume that our habits of mind, traditions, ways of life, and standards of good and evil derive from an all-powerful and wise creator akin to the God of the Book of Genesis who said "Let there be light"—to give primordial order to a chaotic, formless universe—and then proceeded to issue moral commandments after creating man in his own image.

What is certain is that human life is imbedded in moral, spiritual, and intellectual traditions, and values that form a tapestry of order, predictability, and meaningful identities. Still, the original dynamics that explain the exact origin of our communal life-maps are shrouded in obscurity even to the most keen historical and philosophical investigations. Inquiry into beginnings is—like every form of rational reflection—never free of hidden cognitive and value assumptions that direct its ways of classifying, perceiving, and judging. Reflection itself, then, is always guided by maps which both create and populate its territory with objects and places to visit. Perhaps we only discover what we already spawned from ourselves.

It makes good sense to postulate that our possibilities for possessing self-identity, for being moral agents, for conceiving of the boundary between life and death, and for experiencing forms of time, space, and causality—and many other things!—are shaped by culture. Culture creates and reinforces horizons of intersubjectivity—with its typical distinctions between the knower and known, mind and matter, self and other, good and evil, and truth and falsity. Serving as a kind of collective mind, culture teaches us values, cognitions, and judgments that are experienced as "normal." Life comes to have clarity, stability, and a large dose of predictability because culture defines of what the business of life consists and how to proceed in conducting it. Our experience of "reality" arises only after culture gives us detailed maps that enable the world to be separated into distinct regions of "being."

Can we begin to fathom culture's motivations—assuming culture can be said to have "motivations"—for creating typical self-identities, hierarchies of good and evil, and recurring patterns of judging and behaving in the exact ways it has? Indeed, how is mind able to shed the cultural heritage imbedded in language that forms its habits of thinking and observing to find new, unbiased truths about life, self, and world? Even the thoughts of the most discerning philosophers would seem to be wedded to the tacit, regulative assumptions of the cultural and linguistic traditions in which they are imbedded.

The philosophical vocation might best be conceived as a heroic effort to gain clear awareness of things that are tacitly known, that is, to raise these up from inarticulate obscurity to be identified, surveyed, and critically judged by mind's penetrating light. Yet success in this enterprise seems problematic at best, for not only language but our very sense of self and world are based on maps of reality provided by an unfathomably complex set of cultural conditions.

Perhaps the true difference between the philosopher and non-philosopher is that the philosopher struggles to excavate for critical inspection the tacit assumptions that define and regulate a culture's commonly employed concepts and values—be these of God, self-identity, good and evil, human relationships, or ideas of social justice. It appears that most people lack serious, sustained devotion to the philosophical life because economic pressures, family responsibilities, and a paucity of leisure tend to insulate them from developing any strong impulse to inquire into the origin, nature, and meaning of their typical ways of conceiving, valuing, and living. How sad to think that the majority of persons are indolent creatures of convention whose lives unfold in a largely unconscious manner.

Philosophical debates over the nature of knowledge, morality, and self-identity cannot be absolutely settled because these debates are always conditioned by the habits of mind that are distinctive to, and imbedded in, particular cultural forms of life. It would seem that the species of reflection traditionally identified as "philosophy" engenders the paradox of trying to find universal truths that are independent of the ingrained habits of thinking that culture inscribes in its maps of reality. Philosophers vainly imply they are godlike when they claim that thought is autonomous and self-determining, much like God is said to be the ultimate self-caused agent that freely created the world out of itself.

Masks of the Emerging Self

Is stable self-identity possible if every human life is, at bottom, a constant flow of dreams, moods, thoughts, and happenings that arise and depart in awareness for unfathomable reasons? Indeed, madness must reign if the self cannot imbue its life with threads of coherence, predictability, and purpose. And if disorder and madness are hardly typical experiences of most people, then perhaps that is due to the presence in ourselves of that wise and marvelous Weaver that fashions a core self from our cacophony of impulses, feelings, and thoughts.

The prospect of personal identity emerges out of the vast ocean of instinctual drives, feelings, and cognitions only after culture—that marvelous Weaver—intervenes to create divisions between dreaming and wakefulness, between the "I" and the "other," and erects a hierarchy of stable values, cognitive distinctions, and behaviors that enable persons to interact in relatively secure ways. Personal identity expresses what is irreplaceably unique in a particular self's thought and action, and stands in contrast to the aggregate identities that arise from learning common communal traditions, values, and behaviors that have the force of habit.

Only when persons experience themselves as bodies and minds capable of a high degree of autonomous observation, judgment, and emotional expression can their individual characters be differentiated from others—leaving aside the obvious empirical differences of size, weight, skin, and hair color, which tell us nothing about their special moral and spiritual natures. Each self, then, possesses its own "weaver" that gives its existence, to greater or lesser degrees, its own special manner of life that cannot be imitated by anyone else. Still, the expression of unique self-identity is thwarted by the impact of authorities, customs, laws, and institutions that try to secure their own stability and legitimacy by suppressing individual ideas and actions that may introduce disturbing novelties into the communal fabric. Mired in a cultural heritage it fails to create, the self is forced to project its uniqueness in a context that imposes limits and expects obedience.

Once birthed into life, the self's identity is quite malleable and subject to the shaping influences of family, school, and peers as it learns the culturally sanctioned values and practices necessary for communal membership. If the self is to survive and prosper, it must don a host of diverse social *personae* to fit the variety of situations, obligations, and expectations generated in the course of everyday life. Pressured by a variety of duties and standards, the self's identity is easily fragmented and pulled in incompatible directions as it seeks to meet its drives for pleasure, security, status, and scarce goods in an anxiety-ridden, competitive social milieu. As it traverses existence, the self is largely oblivious of the powerful cultural forces that command its life-activity and that create the various *personae* it is compelled to wear to avoid isolation, rejection, and madness.

• • •

Still, the self need not be a mere puppet of forces entirely beyond its control. It has the capacity to detach itself from its culturally habitual ways of thinking and acting to view these with critically inquiring eyes and, from time to time, strike out on its own.

For example, I perceive the world around me as filled with other bodies analogous to my own because these are extended in space, show a capacity for physical movement, and possess properties much like my own, such as legs and arms and—most significantly—a head that sits above its vertically erect body that appears to be the center of speech, emotion, and action. Perceiving these others to be persons distinct from other entities—for example, frogs, trees, boulders, clouds, and water—that inhabit my world, I still cannot say with absolute certainty that these analogies *prove* that organic forms I habitually call persons *actually* possess minds and emotions instead of merely *seeming* to have such.

Because I cannot directly inspect states of consciousness and feeling of other persons, it seems I am fated to remain a spectator who can only infer from an unbridgeable distance that their gestures, words, and actions are the outer expressions of a parallel inner world of mind—the seat of thoughts, intentions, and feelings. The existence of other minds is ultimately a hypothetical judgment and not an absolute certainty. Directly knowing myself to be a center of awareness and emotion in no respect proves that others also experience themselves in the same fashion. If it is true that I alone possess mind and feeling, then everything else I perceive is my own creation—a thought that can drive me to madness. To avoid that fate, I am compelled to assume that others are analogous to myself because their gestures, speech, and behavior *seem* to indicate they also possess minds that direct thought and action.

Attributing to others autonomous and real identities is a powerful cultural and psychological necessity for humans, for how else could I—and you—have expectations about the likely behavior of others unless they are seen to have the ability to speak and act predictably in response to my own words and deeds? Social interaction involves both action and reaction on the part of persons, a fact that implies—but fails to prove decisively-- that separate minds and wills do exist. Still, the fact that I—and others—can raise serious philosophical doubts about the existence of other minds shows that it is possible, to some degree, to overcome the cultural conditioning that suppresses free reflection. The foundation of individual uniqueness stems from the capacities to question, ponder, and to see the familiar in new ways.

———   • • •   ———

A world that depends solely on my mind for its existence would place me in the position of being an omnipotent god. If it were true that I am the sole foundation on which all things rest—including the reality of other minds—then such a condition would prove terribly lonely. I might be tempted to end my misery if I had sufficient courage. How could I bear the terrible truth that everything and everyone that I encounter as seemingly independent entities are merely my imaginative projections?

And I would feel terribly sad and alone if other minds failed to exist, because I would be the only being that suffers from the gyrations of mood and perception that easily overwhelm me with anxiety when my cultural Weaver of stable self-identity loses control. There is a certain solace to be gained from thinking that others have mental and emotional experiences roughly identical to mine; then at least I would not be totally alone in this boundless and obscure world.

There is a vast difference between wanting solace and seeking truth. Is it true that other people have unique selves because they, too, possess special Weavers that knit their various threads of identity into the coherent tapestry we traditionally call "character"? And do they from time to time experience an anxiety similar to mine, born of the troubling thought that their ideas, feelings, and actions fail—when viewed as a totality—to present a consistent whole? Does coherent self-identity actually exist or is it simply a fiction necessary to the sane conduct of life?

It should be clear that the issue of coherent self-identity arises only when persons detach themselves from their variety of life-activities to judge whether these parts form a consistent whole. And the impulse to ponder personal identity arises from a suspicion that perhaps one's life is fragmented, self-contradictory, and on the wrong track. The questions of who one is and what is worth pursuing in life must ultimately be answered inwardly and experientially by each individual. Philosophical debates about the meaning of self-identity are of little help to the individual in sorting out his or her life since such abstract disputes are far removed from the unique dilemmas, issues, and experiences that mark the life of each person. The feelings, thoughts, and perceptions that arise and dissipate in one's consciousness—for reasons that cannot be fixed with certitude—are never identical to anyone else's.

A final conjecture: Could conscious self-identity be little more than a focal awareness that, for uncertain reasons, is catapulted to mind's surface by a powerful feeling, event, or situation that momentarily ensnares attention? Admitting that my conscious experience of self-identity is always altering leads me to think that I have a storehouse of other possible identities that are exiled to some shadowy, hidden region of my mind. Indeed, these repressed identities are locked in a perpetual contest with each other for the right to wear the wreath of victory that signals the emergence of a new but unstable commanding self-awareness.

The victorious one, ablaze in a golden halo of pride, soon succumbs to fear that one or other of its exiled rivals will soon surface from the deep pool of Self to dispute the mantle of rulership. Each strives to gain sole possession of mind and body so that thought, sight, and hearing—indeed, all the senses—become the instruments of its tyrannical will.

Romantic Mysticism and the Real

In strident tones of self-righteous fervor, Charlene Spretnak' book—*The Resurgence of the Real: Body, Nature and Place in a Hypermodern World* (1997)—paints a dark, pessimistic analysis of modernity as disjointed, degrading of human potential, and hovering on the brink of catastrophe. Wearing the *persona* of a prophetess who issues dire warnings to humankind, and striving earnestly to avoid sharing the fate of Cassandra who no one took seriously, Spretnak offers a rather familiar morality play that bespeaks of certain doom unless we heed her vision of salvation from the myriad evils of modern culture. She weaves together threads of black despair and filaments of sweet hope into a biblical drama of three parts: a premodernity of relatively paradisical wholeness followed by the inevitable fall—the loss of a primordial innocence—into the accursed plague of "hypermodern" disunity which, in turn, prepares the suffering spirit to be transfigured by drinking from the healing waters of "ecological postmodernism."

Judging that the post-Cold war frenzy of consumerism, technological innovation, and multinational expansion fails to bring greater freedom, spiritual fulfillment and social justice, Spretnak claims we must reverse civilization's course given the "disintegration in recent years of so much that previously seemed stable." And if "much of the breakdown is part of a larger dynamic," then she thinks that the Satanic power suffocating our lives is a "modernity" which originated from "four roots": Renaissance humanism, the Reformation, the Scientific Revolution, and the Enlightenment. Taken together, these roots sprout the evil flowers of ecological destruction, capitalistic greed, mechanistic and lifeless images of nature, the decline of organic communities, and a male dominated technocratic culture. Copernicus, Kepler, Galileo, Descartes, Bacon, Luther, Calvin, Hobbes, Locke, Smith, Hegel, Marx, Darwin, and Freud are targeted as the arch-conspirators who fathered terribly flawed paradigms about nature, self-identity, political life, progress, and knowledge that evolved into a pernicious modernity of experiences and civilizational aspirations intended to liberate us "from the vagaries of the body, the limits of nature, and the provincial ties to place."

For Spretnak, we are the heirs of largely masculine traditions that suppress the healing powers of a feminine sensibility that would save us from a gender tyranny that fosters alienation, anxiety, insensitivity, greed, competition, and finally, a profound experience of shipwreck.

If rationalist scientific materialism, capitalist enterprise, and expanding technology are tarnished idols that fail to bring spiritual fulfillment and planetary ecological balance, then these forces for Spretnak are responsible for growing socio-economic inequalities among nations and regions, for increasing episodes of ethnic violence, for declining health conditions, and for the voracious destruction of natural resources. Spretnak judges that capitalism and socialism are the twin offspring of the same modern drive to master the laws of nature, society, and human behavior by utilizing scientific methods that depersonalize human cognition and narrow the creative imagination, stripping perception of its inherent power to penetrate the numinous and healing depths of being. The explosion of new technologies to meet increasing consumer demands is the unhappy result of malicious corporate advertising facilitated by a hegemony of specialized knowledge elites that direct the course of public policy largely immune from citizen deliberation and democratic consent. For Spretnak, these elites epitomize the modern rationalist spirit that treats persons, society, public institutions, and the sacred cosmos as objective entities to be manipulated to facilitate a misguided sense of historical progress.

Modern life, then, is portrayed as fractured and depleted at the dawn of the Millennium because the "living cosmos" is treated as inert matter, persons as despiritualized entities, social life as the field of ruthless competition between self-regarding individuals, and the planet Earth as the storehouse of infinitely exploitable resources. Spretnak issues sweeping claims that "modernity" is the soil on which grows citizen apathy, oppressive gender relationships, violent crime, teenage pregnancy, and drug abuse. The bacillus of "modernity" also infects primary and secondary education by presumably suppressing the natural abilities of the young to be creatively spontaneous, to develop holistic, life-affirming values, to embrace spiritualized relations to an organic cosmos, and to nurture ecological-minded local communities of diverse religious and cultural traditions.

——— ••• ———

Much as the ancient Gnostics viewed existence as an unrelenting cosmic conflict between the divine powers of good and evil, with the human soul serving as the primary battlefield in their contest for supremacy, so Spretnak offers a vision of our lives entangled in a struggle between a horrific modernity that spawns every manner of vice and a healing power that would save us.

For Spretnak, matters are indeed dire but not utterly hopeless. She counsels us to listen to the call to renewal struggling for audibility beneath the modern rubble, "the real is poking its true nature through the modern abstractions that have denied it for centuries." That summons to happiness, unity, and redemption is being heard in the current wave of anti-mechanistic cosmologies, in the rediscovery of the beauty and spiritual nature of the body, in the healing arts of alternative medicine, and in the growing desires to create communities of compassion, mutuality, and rootedness. This flowering of ideas and impulses enables us "to increase our abilities to see beyond the boundaries of the modern world view" to be blissfully transfigured, and Spretnak locates the origin of the mystic voice of the "real" in the profound insights and ideals of the "Romantic movement, the Arts and Crafts movement, the cosmological and spiritual quests in schools of painting, the counter-modern modernists, Gandhi's Constructive Program, and the counterculture."

Spretnak's brief surveys of the poetry of Blake and Coleridge, of the ecologically aware theories of Morris and Ruskin, of the mysticism of Blavatsky and Steiner, of the spirituality of Ghandi, and the counterculture protest movements of the 1960's, are intended to enlist these and other *illuminati* into her visionary, apocalyptic army of virtue to justify her gospel that nature, society, and the individual will be healed of every modern malady by deep contact with the truly "real" in the vital experiences of "the knowing body, the creative cosmos, and the complex sense of place." Scripted to perform as a chorus that sings monotone refrains drawn from Spretnak's own musical composition, the rich individual—and sometimes contradictory—voices of these *illuminati* lack true audibility.

The healing music that Spretnak composes for our weary, sick spirits is titled "ecological postmodernism" that she distinguishes from the sophistic rivals chords of "deconstructionist postmodernism," which, despite its largely accurate criticisms of modernity, is fatally flawed for judging truth and value claims to be arbitrary socially constructed "metanarratives." Both the advocates of scientific-technological modernity and their postmodern critics engage in the "repression of the real," the former by fostering on the unwary a constricting objectivistic, mechanistic world-view, and the latter for reveling in subjectivity and relativism. Spretnak affirms an absolutist "ecological postmodernism" to establish her credentials as an inspired guru who *knows* the cosmos to be a living mystical being, who is *certain* that alienation is overcome in the organic relatedness of small communities, and who is utterly *convinced* that modernity spawns the greatest evils because it thwarts both the imagination and spirit essential to becoming whole, organic, and joyful through perceiving that "the earth is the great economy, the great educator, the great healer, the great organizer, the great artist, the great experimenter, and the great blend of cosmic novelty and continuity."

Spretnak belongs to that growing chorus of prophets of doom and renewal who claim absolute insight into the obscure mysteries of birth, death, suffering, historical evolution, and salvation. As the Millennium dawns, many Americans are turning to diverse spiritual teachers and cults to fathom the reasons for, and to find solutions to, their unhappiness and lack of center. No doubt Spretnak's critical diagnosis of modernity is a heartfelt response to the depleted cultural and political soil of our age, and although her analysis contains grains of truth, little is offered that is theoretically new, being instead an amalgam of current New Age thinking as applied to biology, cosmology, ecology, psychology, and community life. She takes her place in the growing pantheon of spiritual teachers who offer a variety of therapies to the anxious, the isolated, and the confused.

———   •••   ———

Spretnak's theorizing about solutions to our communal and personal problems is best viewed as romantic mysticism. Mysticism is an intense feeling of participation in, and illumination by, a sacred ground of being that cannot be shared directly with others because it is speechlessly experienced as a radiant indwelling of spirit. Still, it is unjust to reject claims to mystical insight as utterly irrational fantasy, or, as Freud would have it, as a regression to some infantile "oceanic feeling" that fosters primitive feelings of unity, nurture, and security. It is sensible to distinguish a genuine mysticism from a mysticism of escape. The former consists of ineffable experiences that are personally transforming but leaves the cultural and political worlds largely untouched, whereas the latter affirms that unhappiness, conflict, and evil, whether in the spheres of love, friendship, family and communal life, can be transcended by direct knowledge of a radiant ground of being that infuses joy, love, and security into the collectivity. Spretnak, then, would weave threads of some transcendent ground of being—"the real"—into the fabric of civilization to give us a new life and to solve our many complex economic, ecological, and political problems.

What she advocates is a mysticism of escape that invites a dangerous collapse of ego-boundaries to know a "real" that presumably cures contemporary life of its hardships, insecurities, and dangers, as if these are mere semblances to be transcended by a community of "knowing ones" in bursts of ineffable feeling. Rather than affirm that life is inherently composed of a rich manifold of experiences, from the basest impulses to the most sublime motives and sentiments—and that these entwine as the inevitable condition of being human—Spretnak asks that we flee into the eternal bliss of the "real" to save our lives and communities. Genuine mysticism teaches that we are both infinite and finite, that joy and suffering are reciprocally conditioning, that we share the qualities of both God and Satan, and that the alienation and anxiety of civilization are hardly veils of Maya but indispensable educators that discipline our awareness of unity in the manifold of life's contradictory and paradoxical states of feeling, thinking, and acting.

Spretnak's solution to the illnesses of modernity is hardly unique; rather, she is ensnared in, and blinded by, that age-old powerful drive to abolish suffering and to restore a lost paradise—a "resurgence of the real." Experiencing the "real"—whatever its exact meaning might be!—may offer solace and moments of sublime mystical oneness, but these can neither solve our global political and economic problems nor eliminate anxiety and pain from our personal and collective lives. A paradisical Garden of Eden is forever lost, and with it, the egoless sense of unity of Adam and Eve who, in their total ignorance, lacked the sting of moral freedom, depth of spirit born of knowing division and pain, and a sense of spiritual adventure prior to eating from the Tree of Knowledge, an act which led to their fall from the grace of unconscious unity into a truly suffering human life born of awareness—a life that we share.

The "real" for Spretnak is, at bottom, conceived as a feminine ground of being, indeed, a primordial goddess who reappears in our troubled times to voice the gospel of "ecological postmodernism" to save us from the destruction wrought by the ruling phallic powers. Spretnak's placing the immaculate good in the feminine and the darkness of evil in the masculine is hardly sensible; rather, it insults the truth that the human spirit is a field of tensions and contradictions that plague both men and women and cannot be fully abolished without obliterating the root of life itself. Good and evil are not absolute poles of identity; rather, these manifest not only various shades and degrees but may tragically appear together as inseparable twins, a fact that can cause ethical choices to be painfully difficult if only because living sometimes entails taking decisions that engender both positive and negative consequences. Experiencing Spretnak's "real" will hardly eliminate adversity, injustice, suffering, anxiety, and evil from shadowing our lives, regardless of one's gender, and that is a bitter truth which applies to any conceivable cultural milieu or institutional organization. Paradise regained is not our earthly fate, for life cannot be life lacking the dialectical contrasts of unity and division, spirit and body, reason and feeling, love and hate, and good and evil.

——— ••• ———

It is dangerous to view life as posing simplistic, absolute choices between good and evil. That outlook marked the Nazis who, besides criticizing basic trends of modernity, whether technology, political liberalism, or the Christian and humanistic ideals of love and compassion for the weak, showed themselves to be sordid magicians who, animated by *ressentiment* and an absolutist ideology, transformed public life in Germany into a spectacle of communal transcendence for the so-called racially pure *Volk*, with the consequence of rejecting not only Jewish and Christian moral limits but reason itself by urging people to experience "truth" in their blood, thereby catapulting the German people into war and Holocaust in an insane effort to cleanse what for them was an evil and corrupt modernity. Spretnak's preaching the wholesale rejection of modernity may lead us down a dangerous road that ends in a politics of irrationalism that fails to sublimate the human drive for unity and meaning into plural and tolerant expressions.

Much like John the Baptist, who announced the coming of the Messiah whose "glad tidings' would fill the lowly and suffering with joy and keys to the Father's glorious heavenly kingdom, Spretnak too proclaims her apocalyptic vision of salvation through the "resurgence of the real" that, unfortunately, is a gospel concocted of fashionable refrains drawn from the repertoire of diviners of doom and resurrection that currently populate America's cultural landscape.

Perhaps it is the case that that contemporary civilization is hovering at the edge of a black hole that threatens annihilation unless its powerful gravitational grip is broken; but I fear that Spretnak's teaching will not release us from that danger but might hasten ruin. Rather than flee into the "real" to heal our suffering, anxiety, ecological problems, social injustices, and imperfect political institutions, we should creatively embrace the intrinsic stresses and paradoxes of life with courage and vision, recognizing that joy, beauty, wonder, personal growth and freedom cannot be meaningfully experienced unless ugliness, anguish, limitation, and tragedy are also affirmed as recurring realities of the human condition. Spretnak's counsel that we dwell in the luminosity of the "real" serves death, not life, for life is found in the creative interplay between good and evil, spirit and body, sublimity and horror, love and hate, union and division, and God and Satan.

At bottom, Spretnak offers us little more than a theoretically refined and spiritually enriched 1960s counterculture ideology that failed to create an America free of poverty, racism, gender oppression, elite power structures, corporate greed, unwise military adventures, and ecological destruction. And if Spretnak's "real" is a feminine goddess who would fill her devotees with numinous experiences of unity and well-being, then initiation into her cult requires that her updated New Left political, cultural, and spiritual agendas are passionately embraced as holy script.

The great and timely issues posed by modern life still challenge reflection despite Spretnak's valiant effort to illuminate the darkness and mend our fractured spirit.

(My review originally appeared in an abbreviated form in the San Francisco Chronicle Sunday Book Review section on August 3, 1997.)

Parody of Postmodernism

Am I perhaps a postmodern man or woman, or an androgynous blend of both that obliterates the outworn division of gender identity? Do the words before you fail to convey *my* thoughts and experiences because I, the writer, lack a core identity, that is, an "I" from which definite intentions, meanings, and ideas emanate? And are *you*, my reader—as *is* every reader!—merely a metaphysical creation of an outmoded modernist epistemology and therefore without reality as a tangible someone to whom my writing is addressed?

Or maybe you are not a reader at all, but instead the creative writer of the jumbled texts that dance before your eyes. After all, words lack meaning apart from your own interpretive impositions that continually change with the imperceptible influences of mood, digestive state, climatic condition, and, yes, intellectual and political fashion.

Alas, it is "progress," whatever *that* word might signify to my postmodern spirit, now that the traditional division between the writer and the reader has disappeared, much as when two rivers join waters to become a single torrent that pours into a vast sea where they forever lose their distinct identities. In my postmodern universe anything which exists easily transmutes into something else quicker than a blink of the eye.

Let's face it! I have totally overcome my youthful, immature metaphysical fantasies by being enlightened to the *truth* that no dualities of any kind exist. Hence, I adamantly refuse to erect any untenable distinctions between reality and illusion, cause and effect, inner and outer, subject and object, mind and body, nobility and baseness, right and wrong, self and other, or speaker and hearer.

Ah, what a liberating experience postmodernism fosters in my soul, and in yours too if only you open your heart to receive the new gospel. Every aware person must truly *know* that judgments are always perspectival and relative because words and experiences are never univocal but carry an infinity of possible meanings.

Do not be offended when I say good riddance to Plato, Augustine, Aquinas, Spinoza, Locke, Hegel, Heidegger and the whole rest of that perverse reason-intoxicated flock of extinct philosophical birds. And just as well, for they befuddle the mind by erroneously thinking there is a stable ground of being to which reason can attune to find unconditional, undefiled truth. They fail to recognize *the truth* about truth, namely, that nothing is real except the effervescent play of shapes, feelings, imaginings, and thoughts that stream through us as we wander about the cave of fleeting shadows which alone truly exists.

Indeed, the sun's warmth and illumination, and the void's chill and darkness, are, at bottom, the same. Those who think differently fail to understand that light and darkness do not exist by nature but are merely subjectively imposed categories. To hell with the dualistic artifices of good and evil, god and devil, truth and falsity, beauty and ugliness—to mention just a few—for to set these in rigid opposition springs from an ignorance that erects differences where none actually exist, except of course for deluded minds that have failed to free themselves from culturally hegemonic practices that enchain them in a prison-house of illusory divisions, identities, and ways of life.

——— ••• ———

Whether you like it or not, I revel in postmodern fragmentation, plurality, and relativism because these empower me to issue freely any judgments and interpretations I wish—according to whatever fleeting mood seizes me—without feeling anxiety over whether these be true or false, or to what degree. How gratifying it is to recognize that my ideas and feelings have equal weight despite any superficial *appearance* of logical incompatibility. Besides, I have deconstructed the concepts of the logical and illogical to show that these are entirely conditional in meaning because they originate in context-bound discursive practices that have no claim to universal validity.

You, too, must learn to worship joyfully the great

god of postmodernity that appears to us in an infinity of masks—the *he-she-it* deity for want of adequate linguistic terms—and that breathes into every *he-she-it* androgynous believer a spirit of smiling tolerance that refuses to give rank order to experience, at least once the gospel is accepted that neither nature nor life are inscribed with metaphysical, moral, or empirical truths.

My vitality and freedom grow to new heights the more I make equally justifiable logically contradictory judgments, for I know that life is open to an infinity of interpretations where none are privileged as truth. Hence, I am at once man and woman, born and unborn; and further, upon reaching a ripe old age, I still remain an infant suckling milk from the single breast of my mother-brother-father.

Don't be concerned that my claim violates common sense; after all, we liberated ones *know* that ordinary views about personal identity, gender, and morality are decidedly mired in untruth because these merely convey prejudicial meanings imbedded in specific discourses. Being a plurality of contradictory identities signifies that my "who" is whatever the pure moment dictates as a subjective experience; and hence it follows that I forever alter with the passage of time—assuming of course that time actually exists and its flow is not just a conditional perspective dictated by a particular linguistic game we play! Time passes, time is timeless, time is not: it's really all the same to me as it should be to you, an initiate into the mysteries of postmodernism.

Dear reader: I cannot help but notice the elongated beads of sweat running from your cheeks down your chin and slowly falling to the floor to form a puddle of clear water in front of your bare feet. But wait—do you *really* have a face with cheeks, chin, ears, eyes, nose, and sweat glands as you ponder my *he-she-it* words next to a small pool of water of your own making? Indeed, I am not certain if you actually exist or are imagined, if my words really evoke anxiety in you, if it is I who write these words while awake at my desk, or if the whole episode is being dreamed in deep sleep by another of my selves. Alas, there are only questions and possibilities but no certainties, given the plethora of explanations that are at once true and untrue.

I have accomplished the impossible by succeeding in telling you who I am, namely, a postmodern spirit that forever oscillates between a plurality of self-identities. Although I may from time to time feel debilitating despair when pondering the lack of unifying threads in my thought and action, more often I am joyful because affirming my spirit's fragmentation and diversity makes possible a holy liberation from the harmful metaphysical illusion of having a core identity. Having rejected the Socratic maxim to "know thyself" because intense introspection is hopeless and leads absolutely nowhere, I neither seek unity and stability nor torment myself with metaphysical questions that have no answers. Indeed, I am the quintessential postmodern self, and proud of it.

Postmodern Fallacies 1

Enough, enough! I see the naked figure of Reality walking on stage to have its say. I listen with attentive ears to philosophic music that is rarely heard these days, especially in the ivy-covered halls of Academe where the postmodern deity—the *he-she-it*—rules with an iron fist, and where *his-her-its* minions intolerantly deny tenure (a life-altering fact and no mere subjective interpretation) to those reason-intoxicated—"logocentric"—scholars who refuse to prostrate themselves before the androgynous idol of postmodernism.

The unique voices of thinkers of the highest rank—whether Plato, Aristotle, Augustine, Spinoza, Descartes, Kant, Schopenhauer, or Nietzsche (especially Nietzsche, who would be outraged at being treated as a guru by his fawning postmodern disciples)—are muffled by the clamorous drumbeats that accompany the deconstructive chorus of intellectuals who find their highest pleasure in searching out the mysterious subtexts of these and other philosophers. Their drumbeats are so terribly loud that their ears are unable to hear philosophical voices different from their own.

The all-too-few philosophic masters often sacrificed ordinary comforts, whether stable family life, secure income, or social status, to pursue their mission of pondering the human condition, hoping to cast a few beams of illumination on its ambiguities, limitations, possibilities, tragedies, and vanities. Thinkers of discerning intelligence and enduring value strove mightily to penetrate the dark clouds that dim the boundary between truth and falsity, and to perceive accurately the identity of the world into which we have appeared. They explored the nature of the values and goals that we ought to pursue, and the significance of having brief lives fated to embrace death's uncanniness.

Life, after all, evokes perplexities about the meanings of reality and illusion, wisdom and ignorance, spirit and body, transcendence and immanence, good and evil, self and other, beauty and ugliness, and God's existence, identity, and plan—especially the deity's reasons for creating humans, that strangest of species, who are perpetually shadowed by ambiguity, suffering, and death. Seminal philosophers, then, have sought to experience the illuminating rays of truth to dispel their puzzles, regardless of whether the truth destructively undermined traditional belief to cast people into hopelessness and confusion, proved edifying to a few aristocrats of the spirit, or opened a path to salvation for the many.

―― ••• ――

Postmodern intellectuals often judge the search for truth to be a fruitless task, because for them there is no truth, at least if that concept implies the possibility of attaining universal and enduring insights into the essential and recurring patterns of human nature, social life, and the cosmos. With the erosion of a spirit of truth-seeking, we are catapulted into an Alice in Wonderland world inhabited by fantastical characters for whom every observation and judgment is elusive and fleeting, perpetually deconstructing into something else only to metamorphose magically into a new ephemeral identity.

The postmodern goal is to liberate us fully to be self-determining beings by unconcealing—or deconstructing!—the identities of the culturally hegemonic values, ideas, and interests that shape our self-understandings as sexual, moral, economic, and political beings. The message is that we are imbedded in discursive practices that rest on biased standards for defining the meanings of truth, reason, and morality, and that rationalize as "normal" specific cultural practices and social hierarchies that bolster the privileges of powerful groups—be these political, economic, or gender-based (or the interplay of these). As a consequence, say the postmodernists, inequality, oppression, and ideological prejudice are woven into cultural life; moreover, we are imprisoned by the tyranny of narratives.

But a serious problem arises with this theory. The will to deconstruct is an endless enterprise. Indeed, whatever is deconstructed is itself subject to further unmasking because there exists no ontological foundation that limits analysis from continuing *ad infinitum*. Rational judgment is impossible because nothing can be firmly and finally decided. Further, any deconstructive analysis is intrinsically biased because it, too, is just one interpretive narrative out of many possible ones. Being merely a *narrative about another narrative*, such analysis lacks a plausible basis for claiming that its observations and conclusions are more judicious than competing ones. Perspective piles upon perspective. Every newly discovered subtext quickly grows old and dies, and a fresh one is birthed.

To the deconstructionists, truth as such is nonexistent; instead, there are only prejudices that masquerade as truths. Still, it is one thing to attempt to deconstruct cultural narratives to illuminate the patterns of meaning that mold a variety of social practices and self-identities, but quite another to *justify a rank order of values that infuses existence with experiential richness, purpose, and stability once the hegemonic idols that persons unwittingly worship are rejected as harmful.*

Postmodern thinkers revel in unveiling the hidden biases imbedded in surface narratives, but they rarely offer defensible judgments concerning just *what* ethical standards, institutional arrangements, and social and economic practices can legitimately claim superiority in distinguishing healthy values and ways of life from harmful ones. To take up that challenge would require a courageous act of self-refutation—namely, to embrace the *truth* that judgments are *neither* inherently equal in value *nor* always entirely conventional.

Often claiming Nietzsche to be their founding father, the postmodern tribe of deconstructionists read him to legitimate their own relativism and perspectivism, conveniently forgetting that he, unlike themselves, failed to rest content with unveiling the "hidden history" of hegemonic—and, in his judgment, ultimately nihilistic—philosophical and moral concepts of the Western tradition. Above all, Nietzsche claimed that philosophers of the first rank are legislators who seek to transvalue older tablets of value into new ones; they embrace the *indisputable, non-perspectival* truth that human life cannot survive, let alone flourish, without stable moral foundations and clear horizons of meaning.

He would reject as adolescent naiveté the desire to unveil the robes of Isis to penetrate her forbidden mysteries unless the will to uncover is joined to an equally strong drive to set new boundaries to enable life-affirming values to take root. Without such values in place, external and superior powers will impose their standards and imperatives on persons who lack the capacity for self-command and form-giving. For Nietzsche, the noble, courageous philosopher not only diagnoses and criticizes the moral and spiritual diseases of cultural life, but also acts as a responsible creative healer by assessing which particular values, institutions, and social practices will likely promote well-being for both the individual and community.

"Deconstruction" is a fashionable term, often used by its adherents to conceal, both to themselves and others, the fact that their analytic methods are neither novel nor express a decisive break with older strands of philosophizing. Overly emphasizing the critical dimension of thought but without passing beyond it, the postmodern spirit forgets that great thinkers from every historical period also engaged in deep criticism—even to the point of being destructive—as part of their projects of clearing away prejudice, illusion, and error to prepare the enunciation of truths they judged to be universal, compelling, and unriddling of age-old enigmas.

Kant, for example, who was hardly a postmodernist, challenged the capacity of reason to know the identity of ultimate reality—the elusive *ding an sich*—because cognition always involves the imposition of the subject's categories of space, time, and causality as the presupposition of any possible experience—categories that belong to the nature of the subject and not to the *noumenon*. By positing a rift between how things seem and what they actually are, Kant in his *Critique of Pure Reason* engaged in a corrosive act that undermined the traditional claim, from Plato and Aristotle through Aquinas, Spinoza, and Hegel, that reason is able to penetrate through semblance to the very ground of things.

But Kant failed to rest content with his critical

project. Instead, his intent was to limit science to knowledge of the world of surface appearances, thereby barring it from access to the luminous depth of reality which, he argues, is home to moral freedom and religious faith. Placing morality and faith beyond the rules and proofs of empirical cognition, Kant nonetheless claimed that these embody genuine ways of knowing oneself to be both an ethical agent with unconditional duties and a subject that stands in a personal, irrefutably real relationship to God.

Socrates, too, was obviously not a postmodernist; yet he engaged in his own type of deconstruction, namely, the illumination of largely obscured meanings (subtexts) and implications of the consensual ideas, moral principles, values, and practices the Athenian citizens embraced as conditions of existence. He, too, was a destroyer, because his relentless, passionate inquiries into their favorite definitions of moral concepts and ways of living were intended to reveal both logical and experiential inconsistencies and contradictions—ones that engendered derangements in the *psyches* of the citizens and in the fabric of public institutions.

But unlike postmodern criticism with its theoretically endless unveiling of hidden subtexts, Socrates viewed his practice of the *elenchus* as resting on the defensible premise that truth is separable from opinion and illusion because the deep fabric of reality manifests a stable ground of Being that provides standards, at least to the knowing philosopher, for defining the abiding natures of moral terms, whether courage, temperance, piety, justice, beauty, or virtue.

Whether or not Socrates actually found truth is less important than his search for it. It is likely he thought that destructive criticism is not the final goal of philosophizing, but is rather the essential first step in an epic struggle to clear—through the power of reason—the underbrush of false opinion and untested traditions that conceal the sphere of truth. And knowing the truth would lead to the attainment of wisdom and abiding happiness, not only for the few devoted to the philosophical life but ultimately for society as a whole. For Socrates, then, destruction without creation is an indefensible road for the philosopher to walk, and the postmodern spirit might well learn some lessons from his example.

Although the word "truth" is unfashionable in today's philosophical climate, we still should resist the pressure to embrace today's postmodern spirit of relativism and subjectivism, which, if left unchecked, would silence every voice except its own. Our highest duty as thinkers is to engage in serious dialogues with the philosophical and ethical ideas of the masters in an effort to decide and justify what we ourselves believe, always recognizing that struggling with difficult problems requires radical honesty, for what is ultimately addressed is the question of what standards of value ought to guide our lives.

Postmodern Fallacies 2

It is a serious error to view postmodern trends as evidence of a healthy plurality and a new found freedom of inquiry that happily and successfully dismantles the chains of prejudicial ethical and philosophical traditions. The celebration in postmodern circles of perspectivism, plurality, and liberation from the tyranny of metaphysical foundationalism, while rhetorically seductive, is deeply flawed. Freedom should not be confused with an adolescent reactivity to, and the drive to be liberated from, every obligation and authority, as if these are always illegitimate and conceal the biases of a privileged few dead set on imposing onerous limits on untrammeled self-expression.

Without denying that injustice and oppression perpetually haunt the human condition as dark shadows that cannot be entirely abolished—much as the sun can only illuminate the side of the earth it directly faces while leaving the other part in darkness—it is plausible that the free play of fickle moods and inclinations that spring forth to command thought and action cannot provide a secure basis for a mature experience of freedom. It is simply bad counsel for postmodern thinkers to urge the expression of personal whim and intemperate judgment as the best way to free us from the confining shackles of biased narratives.

The demand that the self unbind itself from the self-interpretations learned from its cultural world carries responsibilities. Defensible moral standards must be decided to distinguish those values, meanings, and identities that merit commitment from those that do not. Also, principles are required to assess rationally the possibilities and limitations of human nature, and to judge which cultural, political, and economic arrangements best serve to minimize violence, promote personal fulfillment, and engender social harmony and good will.

Because postmodernism rejects the possibility of finding universal, common standards, it beckons us to embrace a world bereft of a teleological ground of being—a ground that teaches us to balance limits and form with spontaneity and personal freedom. Unless we discern that balance, both the individual and community are broken into a plurality of incoherent identities rather than experiencing life as potentially fulfilling within a setting of stable horizons.

Authentic plurality needs to be distinguished from what often confusedly passes for it in postmodern circles, namely, *the identification of fragmentation with plurality.*

Admittedly, it would be foolish to deny that, to varying degrees, every human life is a locus of diverse hopes, fears, moods, conflicts, expectations, and activities that threaten to scatter the self into a variety of incompatible identities. There is little doubt that the inherently plural nature of thought and action becomes utterly fragmented as contemporary culture grows more difficult to fathom as a totality, as work tasks are increasingly specialized, and as persons experience their lives as dispersed—"decentered," to use a trendy phrase. Clearly, strong pressures are exerted on people to shift their identities to meet a great variety of social, economic, and familial pressures.

• • •

What, then, are the exact differences between a fragmented identity and one that encounters the natural plurality of life without feeling hopelessly dispersed and anxious?

A fragmented self has a multiplicity of identities that are relatively isolated from each other, and none of these serve as a powerful core that organizes the others into a rank order where each has its proper place and purpose in advancing the life of the individual as a whole. Without consistent threads of identity, the self lacks a stable foundation of values, and fails to give coherence to the variety of experiences, obligations, and activities that mark its life. Instead, its identity shifts in response to changing situations, interpersonal expectations, and institutional demands. Postmodernism visualizes the self essentially as a chameleon that lacks a firm core, decisive will, or overall sense of direction.

Although difficult, it is possible to embrace life's plurality in a manner that harmonizes conflicting demands and experiences. A self can know itself to have a core of basic moral values, life-style choices, spiritual and material goals, and limits and possibilities. Novel experiences, challenging situations, and diverse personal encounters are occasions for the self selectively to enrich itself without feeling hopelessly dispersed. Such a self is marked neither by rigid habits nor fear of change because it knows what things, circumstances, and persons to embrace and to avoid, and to what degrees.

Nietzsche claims that persons are decidedly dissimilar in their capacities to experience life as rich and rewarding, but not primarily because of biased socio-economic and political forces which block some individuals and groups from realizing their full potential. Being catapulted into life carries no guarantee that it will be a worthwhile, fulfilling journey, and that is true regardless of whether one is born poor or rich, ugly or beautiful, or with a propensity to be stupid, intelligent, or creative.

Perhaps it is illusory to think people would be happier, and society less violent and more just, if everyone had relatively equal material resources, roughly identical educational opportunities, and guaranteed quality health care to diagnose and treat their physical and emotional diseases. Although implementing these policies might be judged in some circles to be socially beneficial and morally virtuous, it would be impossible to prevent subtle and overt inequalities from appearing—be these differences in motivation, longevity, happiness, intelligence, ambition, creativity, and the capacity to love. It seems that life entails unavoidable contradictions, paradoxes, and ambiguities that, when surveyed as a whole, pose challenges to survival, to finding clarity, and to fulfilling one's hopes for the future.

The postmodern project of liberation from the hegemony of supposedly prejudicial narratives is ultimately barren because it catapults the self into a world of seemingly endless possibilities, most of which are fleeting, ill-conceived, and incapable of erecting a solid foundation for coherent living. In short, the self is invited to walk down the path of nihilism, because it is counseled to reject the guidance of traditional moral, religious, and political ideals. Lacking direction from any authoritative source, the self is thrown upon its own resources to construct firm horizons for life; and unless it gains sufficient wisdom and courage to give itself direction, it will dissipate its energy, accomplish nothing, and fall into a spiritual darkness that is akin to a living death.

To avert sinking into a self-destructive nihilism, the self must somehow learn the virtue of self-command. That requires saying "no" to some possibilities and "yes" to others. If I am right that postmodernism celebrates liberation as an end in itself, that it legitimates fragmentation as normal, and that it is essentially relativistic in spirit, how can stable and justifiable distinctions be drawn between instances of courage and cowardice, virtue and vice, beauty and ugliness, and wisdom and ignorance?

Absent standards of universal truth, these and other concepts would gain their meanings from a historical culture's particular narratives, or from the subjective whims of the liberated self. There is no idea that both the individual and community can achieve their highest development and fulfillment by attuning to a cosmic order of being for insight into their essential natures and purposes. Although moral, religious, and philosophical traditions can have serious errors and prejudices, the postmodern mentality rejects any idea that tradition is also a repository of sound wisdom about the nature, limits, and possibilities of being human—a wisdom born of eons of trial and error, and a great deal of human suffering.

— ••• —

Allow me to summarize two questionable basic premises of the postmodern project. First, it is claimed that the dominant moral values, practices, and political institutions of every culture, whether past or present, embody the self-interested narratives of hegemonic groups that ensnare the relatively powerless majority into lives marked by inequality, injustice, and oppression; and second, that there exists no metaphysical ground of being, knowable by reason, that secures the possibility of finding standards to evaluate the universal "rightness" or "wrongness"—the justice or injustice—of a community's moral predicates, political leadership, or patterns of distributing good and services.

Given the two premises, it follows that no individual or group, whether powerful or weak, can *actually know*—or be the bearer of—what is universally right. Instead, we are *entrapped* in the self-serving rhetoric of powerful groups that persuades us to *believe* that their narratives embody universal truth and justice. It seems that the postmodern spirit deceives itself into thinking that it is impossible to conceive of an unbiased, genuine good of the whole—a *res publica*.

Let me dig deeper. Deconstructive analysis erroneously assumes that hegemonic cultural narratives always arise from local historical factors that condition the development of particular moral codes, religious beliefs, social customs and practices, group and class relationships, and patterns of leadership and authority. Still, the presence of cultural diversity across historical communities neither proves the case for the relativity of moral values nor convinces me that hegemonic groups always persuade the gullible masses to embrace their elitist, self-serving ideals of truth and justice.

Focusing exclusive attention on the local and unique narratives of past and present cultures leads postmodern analysts to lose sight of what is general and common to all cultures. There exist universal, timeless imperatives that shape the empirical unfolding of both individual and communal life. Persons in any historical culture are always exposed to a range of recurring and common experiences which are neither freely willed nor traceable in origin to the influences of unique local conditions. These general features of human life exist by nature. We are participants in an ontological order of being that at once imposes limits on, and opens possibilities for, existence.

For example, to be human engenders the potential to feel a range of emotions, whether love, hate, envy, anger, fear, or anxiety; to be in a condition of laboring to transform Earth's raw materials into useful products to serve life; to communicate about real or imagined objects of mental and sensory cognition; and to be driven by a procreative urge to create and nurture new generations to ensure the survival of the community. And the human experience of worldliness is decisively conditioned by the intricate design of our body, with its erect stance, bifocal vision, and tool-making hands, and by our possessing a brain capable of developing symbolic language that allows people to share their individual dilemmas and collective problems.

It is a universal truth that every culture must address—whether in the mediums of myth, poetry, religious belief, or even materialist science—recurring metaphysical questions about how and why we came to exist, about the identity of the world we inhabit, and about where we journey, if at all, upon dying. Relativism is refuted—and the postmodern project with it—when it is observed that all cultures, whether ancient or contemporary, or situated in the West or

East, always respond to archetypal questions and problems that spring from the essential nature of being human. These questions and problems provide the enduring bases of thought and action; lacking these, we would no longer be a species with distinctive traits, impulses, and forms of life.

Whether we analyze the cultural patterns of the Australian Aborigines, contemporary Americans, Aryan India, ancient Maya, Trobriander Islanders, or Athenians of the Periclean age—or any other known people—we soon realize that all communities address issues pertaining to peace and conflict, good and evil, love and hate, joy and tragedy, death and immortality, hope and despair, truth and illusion, and spirit and body. Every culture develops traditions, customs, and laws that address the thorny problems of equality and inequality, freedom and duty, and the just distribution of power, status, and material goods.

Of course it is undeniable that past and present cultures manifest fascinating and highly significant empirical differences in ways of being human. Still, observable diversities in moralities, religious sentiments, institutional forms, and economic practices hardly offer decisive proof of the proposition that truth is always context-bound and defined by hegemonic groups.

— ••• —

Unable to pass beyond critical, unmasking analysis to posit new values and goals that are shown to be free of prejudice, subjectivity, and self-interest, the postmodern project ironically recapitulates elements of the very moral, religious, and philosophical traditions it seeks to deconstruct as harmful to the individual and community.

When postmodern analysts speak of liberation, equality, self-determination, plurality, and justice, they not only regard themselves as possessing "privileged" insight into the correct meaning of these concepts, but consciously or unconsciously draw upon Marxist, anarchist, and socialist traditions to fashion their visions of social and economic justice, and political freedom. Taking their political and moral prejudices to be equivalent to truth and virtue, postmodern ideologues refute themselves by undermining the possibility of claiming that their narratives and values are intrinsically superior to those they seek to unmask. After all, they tell us over and over that truth does not exist and that it is impossible to issue unbiased judgments!

The study of cultural diversity leads to greater awareness of the plurality of practices, institutions, moral values, religious beliefs, and economic arrangements that express manifold ways of being human. However, recognizing diversity should not lead us to embrace relativism as an unassailable truth. The challenge is to understand cultural diversities as local responses to the recurring problems, needs, limitations, and possibilities that every organized community confronts. Appreciating differences between cultural communities should lead investigators to make reasoned and defensible judgments about the cultural conditions necessary for people to enjoy more fulfilling lives—politically, economically, interpersonally, and spiritually. That path of inquiry assumes that universal standards can be known that spring from the ontological core of being human. Dialogue about the exact identity and implications of that core are essential if we are to avert the dead-end paths of relativism and subjectivism.

We are a strange and wondrous species that is a perpetual source of perplexity to itself. I fear that the postmodern spirit may utterly stifle that perplexity by enchaining thought to unexamined assumptions, restrictive narratives, and dubious political projects.

It is a curious fact that many postmodern intellectuals who preach the need for pluralism, perspectivism, and relativism fail to see that they worship these as a holy trinity of *absolute* truths. That is likely due to the hegemonic influence of the all-embracing Postmodern Church that suffuses contemporary academic life with a spirit that is difficult to escape. Postmoderns ought to take themselves seriously by deconstructing their own hidden biases and goals. The deconstructor needs to be deconstructed for the sake of truth.

EPILOGUE

Walking My Path

Sitting at my desk on a windy, rain-filled night offers an opportune moment to express my most troubled reveries as these well up from hidden places to be illumined in mind's radiance. Feeling anxious and terribly alone, I wonder if Death maliciously entered my heart-chamber to drum rapid beats of impending doom and to circulate its vile filaments throughout my body to blacken everything it touches. And did I really dreamily stagger to the toilet to pass droplets of pale blood, or was nightmare confounded with reality as the boundary between these receded under pressure of distress?

Whatever the truth, I fantasized that I gulped down two tranquilizers, praying those tiny bluish pills might gird me against imminent ruin. Of course I admit that such drugs unjustly stave off a much needed confrontation with the frightful demons that always appear to the mind's eye when we stop deluding ourselves long enough to permit honest examination of matters of utmost importance. In this instance, the matter is *myself*.

As my troubled reverie grows more intense, and

as my heart throbs irregular rhythms and my body shivers in unison with its awesome cadence that intimates impending rigor mortis, I begin to fantasize what the moment will be like when that blood-pushing organ finally stops. I sporadically scribble words to reassure myself that the whole episode is merely a mind-induced fantasy. Finding it difficult to concentrate sufficiently to sculpt sentences which please me, I cease trying and fall into a twilight state of frozen inactivity, soon followed by immense sadness, tears, and a bout of vertigo.

Admittedly, the streaming tears feel good because they seem to expunge dark thoughts to give a few moments of welcome relief. When the tears finally run dry, I am knifed by a sudden panic that sends cold spasms through my innards as my mind whirls uncontrollably, racing to and fro in step with my corporeal shaking. Background noises amplify into awesome pounding tones as my bodily organs seem to uncouple from cords of muscle, tendon, and ligament that fasten them to something solid.

Paying careful attention to the ripples of rain cascading down the windows as ghostly grayish trees sway in the background does nothing to dispel the nightmarish reverie. As my imagination burns hot, new images dance in my mind. One in particular gains in vividness and power. It is of Max, my suicide brother, who died at thirty-five after suffering bouts of manic-depression and dizziness that psychiatrists failed to treat successfully. His curse was either to whirl through life hysterically or to fall into passive immobility.

When agitated he moved rapidly in circles about the living room, refusing to sit down when asked, as if he feared that some malevolent demon would use the opportunity to seize him and ferret him away to some unspeakable place. Max's hysteric episodes were often followed by lengthy bouts of sleep to stave off the pressures of daily life with which he could not cope, whether holding a job, cultivating friendships, or paying bills. He was a sad person who knew little solace.

I cannot stop thinking of poor Max who ended his misery by shooting himself in the head, spraying blood and brain-matter on his clothes, bed, and walls, and lying in an inert, fleshly heap until Suzy, his young wife, returned from work to find him lifeless. The undertakers at the funeral parlor displayed him in a dark brown wood casket decked in flowers with his upper torso clearly visible, and they did their utmost to cover his head wound with a flesh-colored cosmetic to help us forget his horrible manner of death.

But to no avail; he resembled a wax statue emanating an unearthly greenish-blue aura, perhaps caused by some inexplicable interaction of the lights above his casket shining on his plastered face. The corpse was a caricature of my real brother, indeed, a grotesque model made by some fiendish sculptor who took pleasure in watching us view his evil work. Strangely imagining that I was Max's Siamese twin who dangled next to him suspended from a single pinkish-hued umbilical cord, I thought that perhaps

I, too, would meet a terrible end as our bodies and spirits inextricably entwine.

— ••• —

As old images dissipate and new ones arise in mind's stream, my mother's face presses vividly into the light. Named Jenny, she was by nature a tender, sweet, and utterly vulnerable person. Born in a small village near Odessa in the Jewish pale, she was nine years old when she emigrated from Russia to New York City with many other Jews fleeing from the vicious outbreaks of anti-semitic pogroms and from the turbulence and uncertain times engendered by the civil war between the Bolshevik and Czarist armies in the years following the Russian Revolution. Dropping out of high school to work in a garment factory to earn money, she married Charlie—he was twenty-one and she sixteen—and after getting pregnant with the first of four children (leaving aside the several miscarriages she endured), she was totally dependent on him for economic support.

Over the years my father's kindly and well-meaning disposition melted away—as sometimes happens in marriages burdened with material deprivation and the pressing emotional demands of dependent children—to reveal an angry, defeated man prone to bouts of yelling and to releasing his frustration on his wife and children, sometimes physically. Proving himself to be an ineffectual provider and extremely dependent on Yetta, his strong-willed mother, for emotional support, direction, and money, she in turn used her purse as leverage to dominate his life and family (she also lived with us for many years). You can easily grasp how my father's being reduced to a dependent child in relation to her aroused great resentment in my mother, a perfectly reasonable reaction considering that she herself was in an utterly servile condition and could do little about the situation.

Money always seemed to be scarce in our household, even after Charlie beseeched his mother to dole some out. The real difficulty was that he failed to hold a steady job since he was prone to altercations with his bosses, who inevitably fired him for being loud-mouthed and ill-tempered. Matters were made worse because my mother never earned a dime, having failed to prepare herself for any profession except that of housewife—a quite common condition for poor immigrants to the New World steeped in traditional gender distinctions that dictated that women largely remained at home to raise children while men usually served as the sole breadwinner.

My father's frustration found an outlet in serious bouts of gambling at the horse races, which he always justified by thinking that someday he would make a "killing" and return home rich to lavish material benefits on the family. No doubt his gambling was animated by a belief in the widely disseminated ideology of the American Dream in which poverty is not an unsurpassable barrier to gaining fame and fortune. Rags to riches was not to be his lot, as many others learn who addictively buy lottery tickets, or gamble on cards, slot machines, and sporting events—usually with the result of losing their precious money and falling into even worse poverty and debt.

On the evening before he would go to the local track, he would study the picks of experts in three or four racing newsletters to decide his strategic plan. Unfortunately both for himself and the family, he often chose the slowest nags and, as a result, lost a substantial part of his paycheck, although from time to time he would win enough to sustain his belief that a pot of gold would eventually come his way. The old adage that "hope springs eternal" was certainly true for him.

On occasions when he lost his entire paycheck or the money he borrowed from friends under the false pretense of using it to pay rent and bills, he felt so guilty that he would disappear for several days, apparently sentenced by his bad conscience to exile in some seedy part of town to spend "prison time" in the company of derelicts and other defeated, downtrodden souls. Clearly, he wished to lose himself in anonymity from a sense of shame at having damaged both himself and family. During such episodes, we all wondered if he would return home—especially my mother who, in a panic, wrung her hands, cursed his name, and said she would leave him, except that there was nowhere for her to go.

The inevitable result was that Yetta would herd us into her old four-door bullet-shaped Nash on an expedition to skid row to retrieve him from one or another flophouse. And when we found him, he always had the sheepish look of a naughty child, although there is no doubt he felt genuine remorse. Promising never to bet on the horses again, and asking for forgiveness, he would still begin the whole damned cycle again, as if some irresistible force made him walk the same road over and over.

Trapped in a materially deprived, emotionally untenable marriage, filled with anger at my father and grandmother, and lacking the will or means to break loose and achieve economic and emotional independence, my mother suffered from bouts of depression of such severity that she was institutionalized from time to time in state mental hospitals to receive medication and shock treatments—the latter intended to jolt her from immobility back to an intolerable reality. To this day I have vivid images of her being "taken away" against her will by an ambulance after threatening suicide as she wandered from room to room issuing screams and curses without the slightest ability to carry out her household duties of cooking and cleaning.

My mother and everyone else in the family ranked material survival as life's highest goal. Good books and classical music were largely absent, not so much because of lack of money—other poor Jewish immigrant families somehow maintained a semblance of cultural values and activities—but for the reason that my parents and siblings were preoccupied with their own personal struggles and worries that, found release in flaring tempers, physical and verbal abuse, and competition for attention and scarce resources. Being the youngest of four children, (two brothers and a sister, with a ten-year interval between my sister and myself), I felt that after my parents attempted to abort me—at least that is what they sometimes angrily said to me on occasions when I willfully disobeyed them—that my birth was an unwanted mistake.

Vivid reveries about my suicide brother and my mother, who died several years ago—virtually incommunicado, with advanced dementia—after being confined for twenty years in a state home for the aged and bedridden, have released a torrent of recognitions about the roots of my innermost being. For example, as a child of the working class I am prone to express directly whatever thoughts and moods seize me without much inclination to disguise myself, such as falling prey to displays of ill-tempered lashing out when feeling wronged or manipulated.

Although I am inclined to unabashedly open my heart to persons who pay attention, I am never certain about what they *do* see because their perceptions of me—or of anyone else—are inevitably colored by their subjective dispositions and judgments. Indeed, it perplexes me to this very day why it is that professionally educated middle-and-upper class people judge it "bad taste" to show openly their feelings and vulnerabilities—as if a guarded silence about painful personal matters is more virtuous than breaking down one's protective walls to express who one is to others.

There is no doubt that early on I began to visualize life through lenses tinged with melancholic sadness and even a hint or two of paranoid suspicion. And so it was that when I left home at the age of sixteen to explore the vastness of life, I expected to find that misery and ill will prevailed over decency and kindness. Even at that age, existence appeared to me a dark and futile business that seemed to fit Schopenhauer's vision of life as the battleground of egos—the *will-to-live*. Being that insatiable and blind primordial energy that expresses itself in human strivings for power, pleasure, security, and space in a conflict-ridden world, the *will-to-live* is commanded by the illusion that possessing such ephemeral things would quell its anxiety and fill its emptiness.

Angry, suspicious, and unhappy, I ventured forth and discovered that while most people were self-absorbed, distrustful of strangers, or benignly indifferent, some at least seemed helpful, honest, and sensitive—and it was the latter experience which forced me to entertain the new and strange thought that perhaps my vision of life and relationships was unjustly negative and distorted. Sensing in myself the first stirrings of an out-of-character hopefulness, I very cautiously began unlocking my suit of protective armor in an effort to admit a few rays of bright sunlight, and even fantasized I might soon taste the sweet and healing elixir from the cup of happiness—at least once I discovered its hidden location.

Swinging full circle from my habitually introverted, suspicious self to a polar opposite identity of earnestly trying to be a trusting, sensitive, and giving person, I shed my dark-hued glasses that yielded a landscape colored in gray and populated by surly, threatening shapes, thinking that others would respond in a similar fashion. Fantasies of the joy I might know as a reborn spirit were tempered by my inability to shed completely my deeply ingrained fear that being vulnerable was a suicidal invitation to exposure to mortal danger.

My experiment in trust was most instructive. I learned that life normally fails to pose simple and unconditional choices between being utterly honest and vulnerable and being self-protective and deceitful. However, I must admit that to this day, and sometimes against my better instincts, that I still tend to view people and situations as demanding "either-or" responses. Who knows—perhaps I read too much Kierkegaard!

As I freely daydream, I wonder who I truly am and to where the currents of life will lead me. Beneath my public *persona* as a teacher and writer dwells a perplexed spirit seeking relief from the incessant motions of turbulent currents that threaten to carry me into the ocean's depths to be swallowed up forever. Still, I am not without the will to resist. Being graced (or cursed) with a strong dose of imprudence—perhaps with a hint of impudence as well—I am admittedly not sufficiently selfless to suppress feeling now and then a certain pleasure in stirring the pot of controversy by seeking to unmask hypocrites. In a world of conflicting wills and inequalities, and of fears and insecurities, it is difficult to sustain integrity because that virtue often gets in the way of "succeeding" in the great American competition for status, money, and influence. Too often, personal advancement is bought at the price of compromising moral character by assenting to the self-regarding agendas of the influential.

Standing firm against the current usually entails a cost, not the least being periods of material deprivation and career setbacks; and although life has somewhat chastened me, I firmly believe that increasing the weight of the boulder I push tests my character and resolve. When the heaviness threatens to drag me down, I quickly lighten up, and even laugh and dance, at least when I remind myself that individuals who try to make things as easy as possible by offending no one, by being utterly obedient clones at work, and by walking the straight and narrow to achieve what mostly turns out to be an illusory security often go to their deaths feeling cheated and empty because they never took the risks necessary to explore life's limitations and potentials. After all, if life is ultimately a fascinating experiment—and sometimes a swim in dangerous shark-infested waters—then why not exert real effort to be fully oneself?

Let's face it, prudence is a virtue only for small-minded persons who crave material success, peer approval, and security as the highest goals, as if achieving these frees them from the duty of seeing that they, as everyone else, walk on the razor's edge that is existence itself. As life entails illness, tragedy, disappointment, and death, there is really little to lose by standing firm and expressing one's essential character, and letting things fall as they may!

Human beings strike me as naturally tragic creatures, if for no other reason that living demands a stance of defensive self-protection that carries the obvious risk of evolving into hardness and cynicism in relation to others. At the same time, it is humanly impossible to avoid totally the perils of vulnerability since even the most simple material and emotional needs cannot possibly be met without entwining our lives with others to greater or lesser degrees, whether for food, shelter, work, friendship, or sexual pleasure.

Life, then, exposes one to dangers from others as well as from oneself, and sometimes it seems that whoever designed the world and catapulted us into it made absolutely certain that we are fated to seek our paths between two poles of being—vulnerability and impenetrability. Perhaps it is impossible to find the right balance between the risk that extreme openness entails and the cynical, self-depleting way of life engendered by excessive defensiveness.

As Camus would have it, we are akin to Sisyphus, that mighty but fallen Titan who was sentenced by the gods to the eternal misery of pushing a great rock up a steep hill only to have it fall back to the valley below just before he reached the top to find a healing rest from his terrible burden. The best we can do is carry our burdens with courage and grace, recognizing that we, too, are fated to strive for goals that often prove elusive. And more, we ought to admit that life's greatest reward is found in the struggle to meet the challenges that beset us, for lacking a will to overcome obstacles, there is hardly reason to live.

─── ••• ───

A confessional, meditative writer who would share, without the slightest hint of reticence, his dark and light moods, and his personal history, may cause the reader to suspect that perhaps the author is, in truth, disguising himself behind a repertoire of subtle masks. Sometimes that suspicion is well founded because seeming truthful can actually be a shrewd way to conceal things which best remain unsaid. Believe it or not, it would be a mistake to conclude that my abundant voicing of questions, feelings, and thoughts is disingenuous—if for no other reason than I have nothing to lose.

Nietzsche's profound question of "how one becomes what one is" looms supreme in my life, and leads me to wonder if I can ever truly fathom of what my painful, obscure, and wondrous existence consists. The question that Nietzsche raises about himself is one that everyone ought to ponder. Each life is a fascinating mixture of highs and lows, of beauty and despair, of thorny questions and tentative answers that ought to be shared with others in an earnest effort to help us all find greater clarity.

Although everyone hopes that someone very wise will appear in their lives to lift the clouds of ignorance that hamper penetrating vision, it is usually the case that no single individual will be encountered who, on close inspection, can fully give what one yearns to know about existence. We can only walk our paths into the future with heads high, shoulders firm, eyes crystal clear, and admit to ourselves that we sometimes tremble from anxiety as some obscure force carries us along to encounter persons, places, and experiences that we hardly imagined even in dreams.

Perhaps it is best to admit openly our confusion, emptiness, and even desperation, and not just in fleeting moments of quiet self-inspection away from the pressures and incessant noise of worldly life. Too often, a mixture of fear, prudence, and shyness prevents people from sharing their inner thoughts, feelings, and struggles. They are prone to be defensive at the slightest hint that their counterfeit masks of happiness—the "life is fine and getting better" attitude — are being uncovered to reveal the truth that they, in fact, are truly confused spirits who lack any real clue as to why they came into existence. Ah yes, to survive, but for what purpose?

Allow me to affirm that we are a species that tasted the succulent fruit from the Tree of Knowledge and digested just enough wisdom to be aware of our foibles, to say nothing for the moment of our good and evil. But as Adam, we pay the price of being sentenced to exile from paradise before having the opportunity to smack our lips on the Tree of Life to gain immortality. Actually that is for the best; unlike God, we lack infinite time to think about the stupidity and suffering that was brought into being. Having all eternity to ponder the "why" of a terrible mistake is happily not our lot; besides, the intensity of contemplation is decidedly heightened when one knows it to be of finite duration.

So what exactly does it mean to exist? Perhaps we are akin to leaves on the great Tree of Life that at some uncertain moment will fall to the earth to become food for hungry insects of assorted colors, shapes, and sizes. If life at bottom is little more than the condition of falling in space and time between an unknown eternal above and a possibly hellish below, then I cannot imagine a better way to exist than to examine how other people—my companions in the great descent—cope with that situation.

And what do I see? Some allay their anxiety by believing in a happy afterlife to come as reward for virtuous suffering; others turn away from pondering their falling by seeking their center in what they believe to be the sublime joys of marriage, children, and career which, too often, they come to regret in their very marrow; and still others turn to madness, drugs, and raw sensuality to find that strange solace that the darkening of the mind and senses can bring.

— • • • —

Where, then, do I stand with respect to the great and wondrous issues of love and death? Allow me first to speak of Death, with whom I intimately conversed several years ago after he touched my body with cold, grisly fingers when I unexpectedly suffered a bout of kidney cancer. As he prepared to carry me off to the other side, I cleverly persuaded him to grant me a reprieve so that I might tarry longer to make a final, determined effort to understand why I ever sprang into the light from that vast unconscious domain for which no adequate description is possible.

Fortunately for me, Death was of good cheer, for he succeeded early that very day in collecting his quota of corpses, which meant that he had more leisure to tarry about than was usual for a grim and industrious worker. After pondering whether he would cut me down to add to his harvest—and perhaps a few other gravely ill persons lying near me in the hospital ward—I cleverly told him that I would rather not serve as extra icing on his huge cake of decaying bodies.

Receiving my words in the best spirit, he proceeded to laugh heartily, and added with a sadistic smile that he would grant me some additional years on Earth before he returned to take me away for all eternity—but only on condition that I absolutely refrain from asking him how much time I had before his final visit! Waving good-bye to me, he remarked that the extra time granted would do me little good because the truths I seek are surrounded by dark clouds that creatures one step above the apes can never hope to penetrate.

I imagine that my nearly fatal disease was brought on by an accumulation of disruptive life experiences (leaving aside the effects of cigarettes!) that eventually made it impossible for my body to resist the wild growth of noxious cells screeching for attention from me, their nurturing host. Perhaps you too, my reader—and your neighbor; indeed, the whole human race—already possess tiny seedlings of cancer waiting to sprout their messages of death. Let's face it, robust health may mask a threatening illness that can lie dormant for years before suddenly striking to remind us that vitality and decay are inseparable twins that are the essence of life.

Cancer is both a literal and symbolic malady; literal because cells in the body rebel against their genetic coding by freely multiplying to thwart—perhaps as a rebellious act of vengeance for being programmed to perform specific duties without their consent—the healthy functioning of tissues and organs; and symbolic because life is unthinkable apart from the fact that it carries within itself the seeds of its own physical demise. Indeed, the constant threat of self-dissolution gives impulse to the perpetual human struggle to prevent those cancerous seeds from sprouting weeds that can choke us physically, spiritually, and in our emotional and work relationships.

--- • • • ---

Is it the case that people are reliably untrustworthy, inclined to be self-protective, deceitful when it benefits them, and rarely spontaneously generous of spirit? Even if one says "yes" to the question, and embraces a rather negative picture of the human species as a whole, it still would be quite unjust to blame persons for their frailties of moral character and for placing their individual needs for survival and advancement above mine or anyone else's. And for one good reason: being a person unavoidably means having a body and mind that no one else possesses because these are separated spatially, temporally, and spiritually from the bodies and minds of others. One always protects what is closest to oneself—oneself!

Having our own hearts, brains, skins, limbs, muscles, synapses, desires, emotions, and thoughts makes it possible for us to be distinct beings. The "I" which I am is mine alone, and, because it belongs to no other, it assuredly demands the greatest protection and nurture, especially against those who would thwart my capacity to be that unique "I" which, in the last analysis, is the only true wealth I possess. The same holds true for every person.

Perhaps a strong dose of cynicism and even a hint of paranoia are natural responses to the wearisome problems, personal conflicts, and insoluble paradoxes that life naturally entails. It is always tempting to give up the struggle and fall into a terrible melancholy that paints life only in shades of black and gray. To do so would be a great error, because life is an event with striking and subtle colors and moods. My counsel: Never cease tasting life's fruits as long as body and mind permit, be these excellent food and wine, luminous sensual experiences, or reading an excellent book that provokes contemplation and wonder, although admittedly the last is a rare event in an age when popular fashion fills the mind with a great deal of nonsense that freezes the capacity for earnest thought.

Having tarried in life for many years, the overwhelming evidence for me is that the human animal is not only the most problematic, miserable, and destructive species, but also the most sublime, fascinating, and joyous. Indeed, if we are created in God's image, then we must ask what that reveals about the selfhood of our maker—the eternal he-she-it. Do not be offended if I convey my confusion about God's gender. After all, we live in postmodern times when absolute identities are neither possible nor desirable because every judgment is merely one perspective that has equal value to every other—at least that is what the fashionable philosophers of our present age tell me!